KNOWLEDGE ENCYCLOPEDIA

ART & ARCHITECTURE

Wonder House

(An imprint of Prakash Books)

contact@wonderhousebooks.com

ISBN : 9789354404030

Table of Contents

ANCIENT
& MEDIEVAL
ARCHITECTURE

AGELESS **ARCHITECTURE**

The American master builder Louis Kahn called architecture the 'thoughtful making of space'. Our earliest buildings were so well made that we can still see and explore their amazing remains. Some are so strangely constructed that modern architects have only theories on how they were made.

Inspiration for early architecture came from wars, religious beliefs, and sacred practices. Inspired by their faith in Christ, medieval Europeans built soaring cathedrals. In the east, a closeness with nature led to buildings set in large, entrancing gardens. Ancient Egyptians stored the remains of kings along with their treasures in towering pyramids. Ancient Romans built columns and arches celebrating the victories of the Roman Empire. All across the globe, ancient, and medieval architecture reflects the remarkable stories of human endeavour.

▼ *Built during the Ming Dynasty, the Forbidden City is the largest, most amazing palace complex of Imperial China*

Folk Architecture

In many parts of the world, people still build houses using ancient and traditional designs. For instance, certain barn styles in America were first seen in Europe in the 1st millennium BCE! This kind of pastoral and folk architecture used local materials. It meets only the most basic needs of human beings. It is generally built by local workers, not by formally trained architects. The designs are cheap, dependable and have thus remained unchanged through the centuries.

◄ *Poplar Cottage in Sussex, England belonged to a 15th century shoemaker. In this house only the hall was heated, and the fire burned in a 'smoke bay' (not a chimney). The ground floor was used as a 'shop', while the two rooms upstairs were bedrooms*

◄ *The pastoral Toda people of India live in small groups along green slopes. Their thatched houses are built on a wooden framework in the shape of a half barrel*

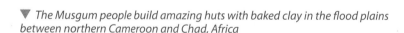

▼ *The Musgum people build amazing huts with baked clay in the flood plains between northern Cameroon and Chad, Africa*

▲ *In Bronze Age Sardinia, people built round fortresses called nuraghe. These were often surrounded by a hive of round stone houses. The whole structure was walled off together as a single architectural unit*

🏛 Climate

Among the most important factors affecting folk architecture is the local climate. Buildings in cold regions are generally thick, low, and covered in insulation. Windows are either small or non-existent. Doors are always tightly sealed to keep the indoors warm. Buildings in hot, dry places focus on cross-ventilation and cooling fixtures, such as screens, gardens, and water features. Areas that face heavy monsoons, tides, or flooding have homes that are raised off the ground.

Windcatchers

Windcatchers are traditional **ventilation** towers of the arid Middle East. The towers often have screens that can be sprayed with water. The water evaporates and cools the air that passes down the tower to the rooms below.

Mashrabiya

Projecting windows (oriels) are excellent ventilators. They are usually formed on an upper storey. In Islamic architecture, these are not covered by panes. Rather they had beautiful lattices and grills to let in fresh air and soft light. Such oriels are called mashrabiya, and they were used in everything from a madrasa to a normal home, and even a **caravanserai**.

In Real Life

The Inuits of Canada and Greenland build temporary winter villages. Their dome-shaped dwellings made of snow-bricks are called igloos. In summer, the Inuit live in sealskin tents.

▲ *The Inuit have over 50 words for 'snow'!*

◀ *Two rows of exquisite mashrabiya at the caravanserai of Bazaara, in a medieval part of Cairo, Egypt. Mashrabiya are plentiful across the cities of the Middle East and North Africa. During colonial times, they were introduced to France as moucharabieh (moucharaby in English)*

Building Materials

Folk architecture draws on local resources. It shows great variety and creativity in the use of common materlals like granite, sandstone, and timber. **Adobe** is one such popular material. It is a heavy, earthy mixture used to make sun-dried bricks. It can be made using clay, sand, silt, and even straw. Another amazing material is cob, which is made of wet earth and organic matter such as hay. The mixture is then rolled into loaf-sized blocks called cobs.

Waterproof structures use thatch and tiles. Thatch is crafted by braiding or packing together dry vegetation. This could be straw, reeds, rushes, heather, or palm fronds. Traditional tiles are made from fired clay. They are excellent for a wide range of climates and purposes. Nomadic people need mobile homes. These are generally made from skins and pelts stitched together as tents.

▲ *A cob building in Morocco; this clay-like material is easily moulded to provide curving structures, and inbuilt features such as shelves and hooks. Windows could be cut anywhere into the wall*

The First Cities

Some of the oldest extant ruins of a city date from the 5th millenium BCE. A prominent example would be Eridu, located in modern-day Iraq. It was home to the Ubaid civilisation. Eridu is known for its numerous temples, made of technologically advanced mud-brick architecture for its era. Most early cities were built during the Bronze Age, around the time writing was invented. City-building began in earnest around Mesopotamia, the Cradle of Civilisation. Mesopotamian architecture consists of the buildings of Sumer, Akkadia, Assyria, and Babylonia. Sumerian cities are among the oldest, and date from c. 3100 BCE.

▲ An artist's imagination of the Port of Eridu

▲ 19th century dig to find the ancient buried Babylonian city of Nippur

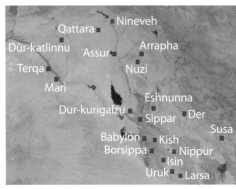

▲ Prominent cities of Lower Mesopotamia in the 2nd millennium BCE

Ziggurat

Mesopotamian architecture is famous for ziggurats which are rectangular stepped towers with temples at the top. Architects used mud bricks to build the ziggurat core. They covered the exterior with baked bricks. Unlike Egyptian pyramids, there are no chambers within a ziggurat. Uniquely, trees and shrubs were grown on the massive slopes and terraces of these buildings. This gave rise to the famed Hanging Gardens of Babylon, one of the seven wonders of the ancient world.

The Ziggurat of Ur

Experts know of about 25 ziggurats in the world. They are spread evenly across Sumer, Babylon, and Assyria. The best preserved is the ziggurat of Ur. It was completed by the Sumerian King Ur-Nammu and his son Shulgi around the 21st century BCE. It is a gigantic step pyramid that measures 64 metres in length, 46 metres in width, and was perhaps over 30 metres in height.

"Bitumen, a waterproof tar, was used in between the layers of brick to prevent water damage"

Indus Valley Civilisation

Around 3,000 BCE, the people who lived near the Indus River (modern-day India and Pakistan) began to build cities. Within a millennium, they had some of the most well-planned and hygienic cities, even by today's standards!

The Indus Valley Civilisation first started off as a farming community or settlement. Slowly, they showed signs of urbanisation, i.e. lots of people started living together in a developed town or city. The civilisation comprised of several towns and cities like Mohenjo-Daro and Harappa. They were based along the banks of the Indus River. The quality of life in the Indus Valley was supposedly better than ancient Europe, Babylon and Egypt.

◀ *Ruins of the symmetrically built homes and streets of urban Mohenjo-Daro*

 # Mohenjo-Daro

One of the largest cities of the Indus Valley was Mohenjo-Daro (Mound of the Dead). On its west was a dominating citadel made of strong mud and bricks, further strengthened by baked bricks. The buildings here included a large tank, a large residence, a massive granary and two assembly halls. The lower town contained regularly laid out streets that led to houses with courtyards. Amazingly, the houses had indoor bathrooms and drains. Brick stairways suggest they may have had upper stories or flat roofs.

▲ *The Great Bath at Mohenjo-Daro shows the Indus Valley people's love of keeping clean*

Isn't It Amazing!

Though they lived far apart, the Indus Valley people and Mesopotamians had commercial, religious and artistic connections. Some experts think that the Indus Valley people built drains and baths to avoid the squalid, smelly nature of Mesopotamian cities!

▲ *Naksh-e-Rustom is a spectacular necropolis (a burial city for the dead) built into the rock face. It contains the beautifully engraved tombs of seven Persian kings, including the great Darius and Xerxes*

The Wonders of Ancient Egypt

The buildings of ancient Egyptians were so amazing, even their ruins are awe-inspiring. They are characterised by massive works of stone, such as formidable walls, gigantic pyramids, and soaring columns. Most surfaces are decorated with **hieroglyphs** and engraved or painted scenes from the lives of ancient Egyptians. This imagery is interspersed with enormous statues of **pharaohs**, mythological gods, and beasts.

▲ Statue of Ramesses II at the Temple of Luxor, Karnak

▲ Painted and carved hieroglyphs at the Dendera Temple, Egypt

▲ Hidden behind the formidable sloping walls of this gateway is the magnificent Temple of Horus

🏛 Great Temple of Amun-Ra

The mesmerising Great Temple of Amun has a dramatic hall of 134 gigantic columns in 16 rows. Each column bears exquisite, detailed carvings along its entire length. In architecture, a hall where the roof rests on pillars, such as this, is called hypostyle—which means 'under pillars'. The design allowed Egyptian architects to build grand public spaces. The temple itself, with its main portion, was designed and built on an east-west axis in line with a dock. This dock dried up long ago, though it was reportedly around 100 metre from the Nile river.

◀ Statue of Hatshepsut, the queen who dressed as a man and ruled Egypt in the 15ᵗʰ century BCE

▲ Another set of massive statues of Ramesses II sit regally at the entrance to the Temple of Luxor, Karnak

⭐ Incredible Individuals

High Priest Imhotep was chief minister to King Djoser of Egypt about 5,000 years ago. He designed and built the first pyramid called the Step Pyramid at Sakkara. Imhotep was part of "The Eye of Horus"—the School of Mysteries that guarded Egypt's knowledge.

▶ Djoser's step pyramid at Sakkara

The Temples of Abu Simbel

Abu Simbel is the complex of two temples built by Ramesses II (ruled 1279–13 BCE). Four gigantic statues of him grace the entrance to the main temple. The temple itself was built to honour the sun gods Amun-Re and Re-Horakhte. It consists of three halls extending for 56 metre into a cliff. These contain statues of the king as Osiris, the god of the afterlife, and paintings of battles. Two days of every year, the first rays of the sun glide through the entire length of the temple and light up the innermost shrine. In the 6th century BCE, Greek adventurers graffitied the sculptures at the temple entrance. This was a gift to experts unearthing the history of the alphabet, especially in relation to Egyptian hieroglyphics.

▶ The 20 m high figures of Ramesses at the entrance to Abu Simbel; around the feet are figures of his mother Muttuy, his queen Nefretari, and his children

 The Temple of Hatshepsut

Built by architect Senenmut in the bay, the temple is named after a powerful female pharaoh. The temple was built in c.1473 BCE on three levels, with rows of colonnades and courts. The path to the temple came up the valley through an avenue guarded by sphinxes. The front court was made into a garden of lush trees and vines. Images on the temple walls show stories and scenes from ancient Egypt, such as the marriage of Queen Ahmes to the god Amun-Re and the birth of their child Hatshepsut.

▲ Deir el-Bahari at Hatshepsut's temple in Egypt

In Real Life

In the late 1960s, Egypt built the Aswan High Dam on the River Nile. This flooded the land nearby. To prevent ancient Egyptian temples from being submerged, many of them—including Abu Simbel—were moved to other places. In fact, the 2nd-century BCE Debod Temple was shifted entirely out of the country. It now sits on a hill in Spain!

The Pyramids of Giza

The three iconic pyramids of Egypt were constructed during the Fourth Dynasty (c. 2575–2465 BCE). They were named Khufu, Khafre, and Menkaure, after the kings who built them. They are made of limestone blocks. They have inner passages and burial chambers for royalty. The pyramid of Khufu is also called the Great Pyramid. It is the oldest of the group, and the largest pyramid ever built. The pyramids were originally covered in white limestone with golden capstones. But over the years, this was hauled away by people to build their own homes. The pyramids no longer shine in the desert sun, as they once did.

▶ Smaller pyramids around the three giants of Giza are burial monuments for other members of the Egyptian royal family

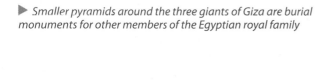

Classical Greece

Greek monuments from 1500–350 BCE are known as Classical architecture. The most famous Classical buildings came after 460 BCE. They are part of the golden age of architecture. Among them are gems such as the Parthenon, the Artemis, the Theatre of Epidaurus. Classical architecture has elements such as friezes, columns, pediments, and caryatids.

▲ *A pediment is a narrow triangle just below the roof. Often, it is a platform for decorations called friezes. Here, you see one corner of the pediment of the Parthenon temple. It has a sculpted frieze of a fallen horse and warrior*

▲ *Caryatids are stone columns in the form of robed maidens. The most famous caryatids are found on the porch of the Erechtheion in the Acropolis*

The Acropolis

Greek city centres were built on high ground, to make it difficult for enemies to attack. This centre was called the acropolis. It held all the chief government and religious buildings. The acropolis at Athens was built during the latter part of the 5th century BCE. Dedicated to Athena, the goddess of wisdom and war, it is located on a craggy, walled hill.

▲ *The modern-day ruins of Athens' acropolis*

In Real Life

Take a look at the capital (the top) of a Greek column. If it is without any decoration, it is a Doric pillar. If it has a pair of horizontal scrolls, it is an Ionic pillar. If there are beautifully furled sets of leaves, it is a Corinthian column.

Doric   Ionic   Corinthian

▲ *Types of capitals*

▲ *The iconic Greek Parthenon at Athens is the Goddess Athena's chief shrine*

The Temple of Artemis

One of the seven wonders of the ancient world, the Temple of Artemis at Ephesus was originally built by King Croesus of Lydia, in 550 BCE. In 356 BCE, it was burned down by an arsonist called Herostratus, who just wanted to scorch his name into history. The temple was rebuilt using the original designs. Alexander the Great offered to pay for this work, but the citizens refused him and used their own jewellery to fund the building. It was finally destroyed by invading Goths in 262 CE. The Temple of Artemis was famous for its gargantuan size (about 110 x 55 metres) and for many magnificent artworks.

The Temple of Artemis became quite popular in the Renaissance of Europe. There was a coloured engraving prepared by Martin Heemskerck that imagined the temple during the 16th century. In the present day, only a single column remains of the temple, along with other fragments near the site.

▲ *Ruins of the Temple of Artemis in Turkey*

◀ *The Ephesus Artemis was a unique avatar of the goddess, made of gold, ebony, silver and black stone. A 1st century Roman copy shows her with a high headdress, a multitude of breasts and dressed in a garment with bee motifs*

Theatre of Epidaurus

The merchant city of Epidaurus once honoured Asclepius, the god of healing, with a magnificent temple complex. It held temples of Asclepius and Artemis, a stadium, gymnasiums, baths, a hospital and an **abaton**. Its open-air theatre remains an amazing feat of engineering. This is one of the first all-stone Greek theatres ever built. The semi-circular structure is 118 metres in diameter and has 55 rows that can seat up to 13,000 people.

▲ *The theatre of Epidaurus is designed in three parts: the auditorium (seating area), the orchestra (the 'dancing floor' or stage), and the skene (a building behind the stage)*

⊙ Incredible Individuals

The labyrinthine palace at Knossos with its paintings of bulls probably gave rise to the myths of the Minotaur—the half-man, half-bull son of Pasiphae, wife of King Minos. The Greek hero Theseus was loved by King Minos's daughter. She gave him a spool of thread to mark his way around the Labyrinth. Theseus killed the beast and freed the Athenians, before leaving the island with the King's daughter. King Theseus was the mythical founder of Athens and was compared to the likes of Heracles and Perseus. Athenians held Theseus in great regard, considering him to be a believer of reform. He was also credited with the unification of Athens and Attica.

The Palace of King Minos

Knossos was the centre of an artistic Bronze Age civilisation. The palace here was once a maze-like complex with numerous pillars and stairways. The walls were painted with vibrant frescoes of dancers, dolphins, and bulls. The entire area was serviced by carefully built drainage and road networks. Inside the palace, the **gypsum** throne of the kings of Knossos can still be seen.

▶ *Painting of a bull at the ruins of the palace at Knossos, Greece*

Classical Rome

In the 1ˢᵗ century CE, Rome defeated and took charge of Greece. At the time, it also took Greek culture to heart. With its advanced technologies, Rome was able to take Classical architecture to its peak. The Roman Empire drew architects, masons, craftsmen and ideas from several other civilisations. The result was an explosion of wondrous constructions that reflected wealth and power.

Arches

The development of arches—a feature that can bear great weights—allowed Rome to build massive and multi-level structures. Arches were used in aqueducts, public buildings, and even in monuments celebrating great battles.

▲ *The Arch of Constantine (312 CE) was built in memory of a victorious battle. However, most of its sculptures are not original but were taken from older Roman buildings. These included panels, roundels, and figures of captives from the time of emperors Domitian, Trajan, and Hadrian*

▶ *The Colosseum is a giant public amphitheatre with enormous rows of arches at every level. It could host thousands of Roman spectators, who came to witness fights that featured gladiators, slaves, and wild animals*

The Pantheon

An iconic Roman temple, the Pantheon was built and rebuilt by several Roman emperors from 27 BCE onwards. It is a circular monument of concrete with a giant dome. The front entrance lies behind tall Corinthian columns. The gates are formed by huge double doors, 27 metres high and made of bronze—the first of their kind. Inside, the Pantheon is lined with coloured marble, granite and semi-precious purple **porphyry**.

▲ *The Pantheon's entrance shows dignified lettering above the columns—an element of proud Roman architecture*

 ## Urban Rome

Most Roman towns began as well-planned settlements. There would be two main roads, heading north-south and east-west. Public buildings at the centre included markets, the town forum, public baths, arenas, military **barracks**, and temples. Many towns also had aqueducts and primitive sewer systems. However, as the empire grew, and towns became cities, town planning was replaced by dirty, noisy urban sprawls, and traffic-choked roads.

 ## Thermae

Roman public baths (thermae) had different types of bathing and storage chambers. There was the *apodyterium* (the locker room), the *tepidarium* (a warm baths), *caldarium* (a hot baths), and *frigidarium* (cold).

▲ *Leptis Magna in Libya has well-preserved thermae from the reign of Emperor Hadrian (c. 117–138 CE)*

 ## A Rock-cut Treasury

The Treasury (Al-Khazaneh) of the mysterious city of Petra (in Jordan) is actually a spectacular tomb cut into a rock face. Originally a **Nabatean** structure, it was remodelled to Roman tastes after its conquest in 106 CE.

They notably added the spectacular Corinthian columns and pediments. The wonderful sunset colour of this rock gives Petra its other name, the rose-red city.

▶ *The amazing Library of Celsus was the third richest library of its time. Its grand facade shows decorated, rounded pediments—a step up from the Greek triangular structures*

 ## Trajan's Column

This 38-metre-high marble column was erected during 106–113 CE by Emperor Trajan. It is a record of fierce wars that took place between Rome and Germanic tribes. The writing and about 2,000 carvings spiral up the entire length of the column. The **pedestal** contains a chamber that was Trajan's tomb.

▶ *Trajan's Column*

Byzantine Splendour

At the age of 52, the Roman emperor Constantine I moved away from Rome. He built a new capital in the east and called it Byzantium. After his death, it became famous as Constantinople (now Istanbul). Constantine was also the first Roman emperor to convert to Christianity. His powerful support allowed Christians to make buildings—both secular and religious—that were inspired by their faith. These amazing early Christian works are recognised as Byzantine architecture.

▲ Byzantine architects combined eastern and western designs. Many buildings, such as the spectacular St Mark's Basilica, Venice, had eastern-style domes

The Hagia Sofia

The landmark of Constantinople is the Hagia Sophia (Church of Divine Wisdom). It was built around c. 532–537 CE by Byzantine emperor Justinian I. For almost a thousand years, it was Christendom's largest cathedral. After a couple of earthquakes partly destroyed it, Tradt, the chief architect of the Bagratuni Dynasty in Armenia rebuilt the cathedral in its current form.

▼ The Hagia Sophia Basilica is arranged lengthwise with a central building. The huge saucer-like 32-metre dome (second-largest in the world, after the Pantheon's) is supported by twin semi-domes

▲ St. Mark's Basilica shows Byzantine elements such as golden mosaics and thoughtfully placed windows. Sunlight would bathe the mosaics and give the church a holy atmosphere

St Basil the Blessed

One of the most recognisable landmarks of Russia is the multicoloured, nine-towered Cathedral of St. Basil the Blessed. It was built to celebrate Tsar Ivan IV's victory over the Tatars (Mongols). This cathedral is the only Byzantine construction of its millennium. It was built over c.1554–60, by when the Byzantine era was long over in western Europe.

An Asymmetrical Gem

The Cathedral of St Basil is built in eccentric shapes. It is formed by eight chapels surrounding a central ninth chapel. This central chapel—the Church of the Intercession of the Mother of God—has a tall, tent-like tower for a roof. The four largest domes sit on top of octagonal towers. These domes cover the Church of St. Cyprian and St. Justina, Church of the Holy Trinity, Church of the Icon of St Nicholas the Miracle Worker, and the Church of the Entry of the Lord into Jerusalem. The **motley** roofs rise to a spire from an onion-shaped dome.

▲ *The Cathedral of Vasily the Blessed, or Saint Basil's, in the Red Square in Moscow, Russia*

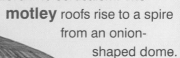

▲ *The lavish interior at St. Basil*

The Holy Fool

The cathedral's name comes from the Russian holy fool Vasily Blazhenny (St. Basil the Blessed) who was a 'fool for Christ'. He is buried in the church vaults.

👤 In Real Life

The site of the Hagia Sophia was first occupied by a pagan temple. It later became the site of Constantine I's cathedral Megale Ekklesia. And still later, Justinian's Hagia Sophia. In 1453, Ottoman Sultan Mehmed II converted the Hagia Sophia into a mosque. In 1943, the Turkish Republic's first president made the Hagia Sophia a secular building. It is now no longer a temple, church or mosque, but a museum.

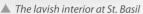

Chinese Architecture

China is geographically vast, culturally diverse and historically rich. In comparison, its architecture shows little variation. This is because, from very early on, imperial governments set codes and standards for buildings throughout the nation. They were also influenced by **Confucian** and Buddhist philosophies.

 Dragons are found everywhere across China—in wood, jade, stone, and ceramic. They were seen as a symbol of royalty. Anyone else who dared use dragons could be put to death as a criminal

▲ The Yungang Grottoes are 53 caves with exquisite carvings of gods and demons. They were built into sandstone cliffs by Buddhist monks over 50 years during the 5th century

Structure and Order

Chinese people often lived in large families. So, Chinese homes had a number of buildings. These buildings were located in a single enclosure with one or more courtyards. Important buildings, such as ancestral and religious halls, would face the front of the property. Servants' rooms, storage houses, and kitchens were kept at the farthest sides.

The Great Wall

You could say all of China is an enclosure. The First Emperor of China built the first Great Wall. Later emperors maintained and added to the wall. What you see now is in fact a series of walls running from northern China to southern Mongolia. Often there are multiple walls running parallel to each other.

The wall was built from whatever building materials were locally available. This included wooden boards, bricks, rubble, rocks, and stones. The outside parapet is generally **crenellated**. The inside part of the wall is lowered, to stop people and horses from accidentally falling off the edge.

▶ The Great Wall of China in the mountains near Beijing— signaltowers were built for storage, to house people and horses, and to send military signals

🏛 The Forbidden City

China's main palace lies in a massive walled-off area in Beijing. It is called Zijin Cheng (the Forbidden City). It is divided into the Outer and Inner Courts. The Outer Court occupies the southern area. It was used for public and ceremonial functions. Its most important buildings also face south, to honour the Sun. The Inner Court contains the palaces of the emperor and his family. You can tell how important a building is by its height, width, style of the roof and the number of figurines on the roof.

▲ Beyond the main gate lies the Golden River, which runs across a vast courtyard. The Gate of Supreme Harmony lies at the end of the courtyard. It leads to the Outer Court

▲ Palace of Tranquil Longevity in the Forbidden City, the palace of the Chinese emperor

▲ Having 10 mythical beasts on the roof indicates that this building (the Hall of Supreme Harmony) has the highest status in the whole empire

🏛 Potala Palace

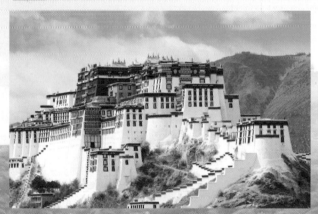

Tibetan architects took Indian and Chinese elements and changed them into an entirely unique style. The Potala Palace—the official home of the Dalai Lama—is an example of this rare architecture. Covering a massive 36 hectares, it contains 1,000 rooms and 10,000 shrines. The building rises 117 metres above a hill. It is a stepped construction of stone and timber.

◀ Every year, the palace is repainted using a special mix made of milk, honey, sugar, white lime, and some herbs. It used to take a whole month to make it, but now takes ten days

ⓧ Incredible Individuals

Thousands of slaves, prisoners, soldiers, and local people gave their lives to build and rebuild the Great Wall. Many of them lie buried in the wall, which has long been seen as a symbol of oppression and tyranny. What is worse, the wall did not stop the invaders.

Islamic Architecture

From the 7th–17th century, Islamic architecture spread across Asia, Africa, and Europe. Muslim architects were forbidden by holy law to show the image of God or living beings in their creations. Thus, they created buildings without statues and murals. Instead, they focussed on symmetry, tile-work and **calligraphy**. Their utterly amazing buildings include the Dome of the Rock, Samarra's Great Mosque, Cordoba's Great Mosque, Topkapi Palace, and Fatehpur Sikri, to name a few.

Jerusalem's Dome of the Rock

▲ *Qubbat al-Sakhra (Dome of the Rock)*

Built over the rock from which Prophet Mohammad rose to heaven, the Dome of the Rock is one of Islam's earliest monuments. The octagonal structure shows Syrian Byzantine influence. It has Roman columns and intricate **mosaics**.

▶ *Samarra's Great Mosque was once the largest mosque in the world. It has a spiralling minaret and is supported by semi-circular towers. Its enormous **arcaded** courtyard can hold 80,000 people*

An Umayyad Dynasty Mosque

The glorious Great Mosque at Córdoba is best known for its amazing prayer hall. It has 850 granite, jasper and marble columns. These support striped horseshoe-shaped arches. Sunlight and lamp-light filter through, casting hypnotic patterns across the floor.

▲ *Cordoba's Great Mosque took 200 years of construction to complete*

Standalone Minarets

In Islam, a muezzin calls the faithful to prayer from the balcony of a minaret, five times a day. Among the tallest minarets in Asia is the 72.5-m-high Qutb Minar. It is a tapering, richly carved sandstone tower. Each floor shows projecting balconies. Exquisite marble work covers the base.

Minarets have a base, cap, shaft and a head. They are seen in many grand mosques, like the Great Mosque of Testour. Minarets are also seen in the Taj Mahal.

▲ Qutb Minar, Delhi

▲ Filigree screens added elegance to windows, arches, verandas and other palatial structures. The filigreed balcony above this wooden column bore the throne of Emperor Akbar at Fatehpur Sikri, India

Taj Mahal

A perfectly symmetrical layout of domes, arches, and minarets in white marble makes the Taj Mahal a marvel of Islamic-Indian architecture. Inside, the **mausoleum** is octagonal. It has ornate carvings and floral designs. These are set in semiprecious stones, such as lapis lazuli, jade, crystal, amethyst, and turquoise. Two buildings of red sandstone stand on either side of the mausoleum. At the southern end is a red and white gateway with arches and cupola. These structures offer a striking contrast to the white marble tomb.

▲ The Taj Mahal is set in classical Mughal gardens. These feature waterways, fountains, ornamental trees and walking paths

Alhambra

The fortress palace of Alhambra is one of the finest achievements of the Spanish Moors. It is set on a lush plateau overlooking a steep ravine. The land is planted with oranges, roses, myrtle, and other fragrant and ornamental plants. Within the fortress are grand courts, palaces, a throne room, fountains, columns, and halls.

▲ The home of 30 Ottoman sultans, Topkapi Palace shows the multiple influences of an expanding empire. It is built in Islamic, Ottoman, and European styles. Its pointed arches became a standard feature of Gothic architecture in Europe

▼ Moorish poets described the fortress of Alhambra as a 'pearl set in emeralds', referring to the amazing colours of its palaces and woods

Architecture of the Indian Subcontinent

Ancient and medieval India created some of the most enthralling architecture in the world. This was influenced by Hindu, Buddhist, Jain, Sikh, Islamic, and many other philosophies. The buildings celebrate nature and the supernatural. They show worldly pleasures and otherworldly pastimes. Above all, they reflect a love for divinity. To share such an abundance of stories, Indian architects built vast, maze-like, and intricately decorated monuments. It can often be hard to figure out where to start exploring or what to look at first!

▶ *The Meenakshi Temple at Madurai in southern India has 14 multi-storied gopuram (towering gateways) packed with incredible statuary. The four largest gopuram serve as the main gateways into this labyrinthine temple*

▶ *Harmandir Sahib, more popularly called the Golden Temple, is the chief gurudwara of Sikhs. Built in marble and copper, it is most notable for its gleaming gold-foil facade*

Tiered Towers

Many Indian temples are built with towers called *shikhara* or *vimana*. They are usually seen rising above the sanctuary or pillared halls. A *gopuram* is a soaring pyramid-like gateway to the temple. Almost all towers have multiple layers. On the outside, they are carved with scenes from legends and local history. The inner walls are sometimes decorated with murals.

▼ *This rooftop belongs to the monolithic temple of Kailasha. It is a part of 34 monasteries and temples cut into a cliff face at Ellora. These shrines show Buddhist, Hindu, and Jain styles*

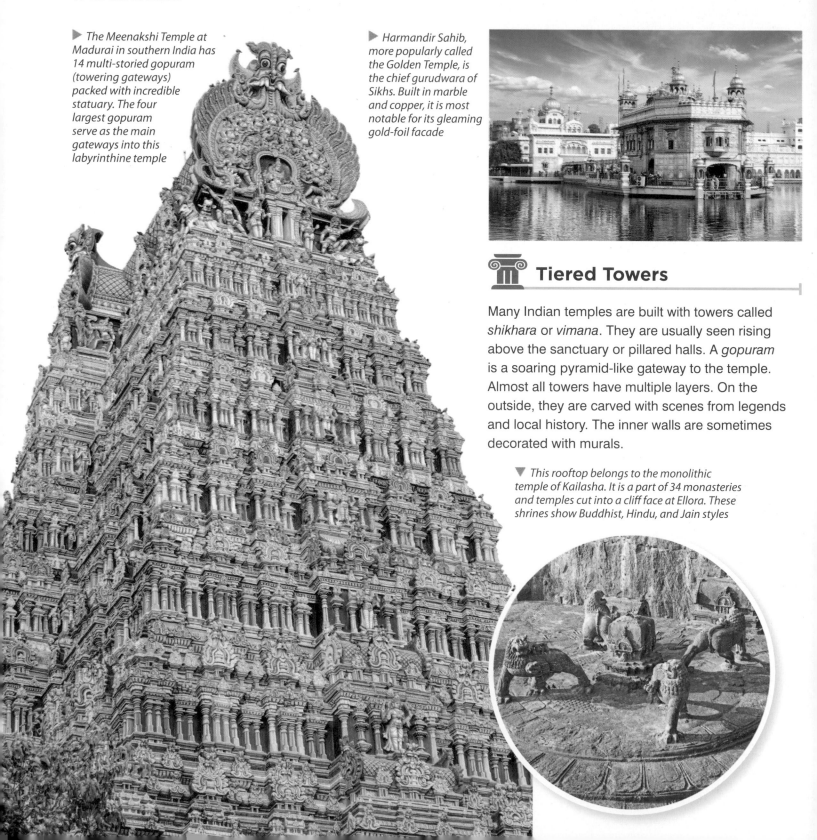

Stupa

Often seen in Buddhist and Jain architecture, stupas are large domes that sometimes house sacred relics. The most famous one is the Great Stupa at Sanchi, which was built by Mauryan emperor Ashoka to honour the Buddha. The monument has four gateways, richly carved with scenes from the *Jataka Tales* and the life of the Buddha.

Hoysala Architecture

The Hoysala Empire's unique architectural style is marked by attention to symmetry and detail. Located by the Kaveri River, the Chennakeshava Temple at Somanathapura is an excellent example. Its *trikuta* (three-shrine) complex is built in a 16-point star shape and is teeming with figurines.

▲ *The Great Stupa at Sanchi is one of the oldest stone structures in India*

◀ *Shrines at Chennakeshava sit on raised platforms, a common Hoysala feature. Each shrine has its own vimana*

◀ *There are several reliefs and wall carvings on the walls of the Hoysala Temple. They depict various scenes from Hindu lore, including battles between the Hindu gods, important events, etc*

Isn't It Amazing!

Emperor Ashoka came to the throne when Buddhism was still new to the world. After one of his victorious but bloodiest wars, the emperor was overcome with remorse for the carnage he had caused. He determined never again to raise arms and instead to conquer using compassion, mercy, and non-violence. He upheld Buddhist values and helped spread it across the land.

▶ *The symbol of the four lions is used on Indian currency*

 ## Pillared Places

Pillared corridors and chambers are a hallmark of Hindu architecture. A *mandapa* is a pillared hall. The most awe-inspiring *mandapa* are built just outside the sanctuary or in between shrines. An *ardha-mandapa* is a porch-like entrance to some temples. *Bhoga mandapa* is used to prepare food for the gods in certain temples. *Nata mandapa* is a dance hall, seen in palaces and temples.

▶ *The shrines of many large temples are surrounded by never-ending, stone-pillared corridors, as seen in the Sthanumalayan Temple of Suchindaram, in southern India. The corridors were lit up (in the evenings) by lamp-bearing maidens carved on the columns*

Heritage of Southeast Asia

The architecture of Southeast Asia shows strong Buddhist and Hindu influence. Indian elements such as the *stupa*, the *shikhara,* and the flower and animal motifs rapidly spread across Myanmar, Thailand, Cambodia, and Indonesia. Architects of these regions added their own creative touches and gave birth to breathtaking new designs.

▲ Rich and massive spires were always loved in Southeast Asia. These are seen at Myanmar's Shwedagon Pagoda, where many gold pagodas surround a 113-metre-high spire

▲ Southeast Asia is a melting pot of cultures. In central Thailand, you can see the Theravada Buddhist temple Wat Amon Yat (left) alongside a Chinese folk-religion temple (right)

Borobudur

The gigantic and extraordinary Buddhist monument of Borobudur was built in Java over 778–850 CE. It is created to resemble Mount Meru, a holy Hindu mountain. Borobudur's form is symbolic of the *mandala*—a symbol of the universe that uses squares for the earth and circles for heaven. The entire structure is festooned with stupas and statues of the Buddha.

▶ The stone blocks of Borobudur express religious and secular scenes. This relief shows the king and queen granting an audience to their subjects

Enlightenment at Borobudur

Built from volcanic stone, the pyramid-like Borobudur encloses a hillock. It consists of three main levels, divided into nine lesser levels. There is a square base, five square terraces in the middle, and three circular terraces on the upper level. The central stupa is 35 metre in height. Each level represents a stage on the path to enlightenment. A pilgrim enters from the eastern staircase, then mimics the spiritual journey by walking clockwise up the levels to reach the top. The total distance is more than 5 kilometres!

▲ The Karma-vibhanga carving at Borobudur expresses the Buddhist belief that those who harm living beings—even such mute creatures as turtles and fish—will be punished in hell

▲ The steep stairway at Borobudur leads pilgrims to Kamadhatu (realm of desire). From here, pilgrims move to Rupadhatu (realm of forms and shapes) and to the highest planes of Arupadhatu (realm of formlessness)

Angkor Wat

Built in the 12th century by King Suryavarman II, Angkor Wat marks the pinnacle of the Khmer Empire's architecture. It is the largest religious complex in the world. Spread across 160 hectares, it is laid out according to the Hindu temple-mountain plan. The temple has five central towers that represent the peaks of Mount Meru. The mountain is surrounded by a vast and complex moat that symbolises the mythical 'ocean at the edge of the world'. One enters Angkor Wat by crossing a 188-m-long bridge. On the way to the temple are three galleries, separated from each other by paved walkways.

◀ *Angkor Wat surrounded by the moat representing the world ocean. Angkor Wat was intended by King Suryavarman II to be the resting place for his mortal remains. The holy images covering its walls include the much-admired Churning of the Ocean, which depicts Vishnu in his Kuruma avatar, surrounded by gods and demigods*

Religious Motifs

Angkor Wat is dedicated to the gods Brahma, Vishnu, and Shiva. It is filled with Hindu motifs. The walls have sculptures of exquisite quality. These depict scenes from ancient Khmer (modern Cambodia) as well as scenes from the heroic Hindu epics *Mahabharata* and *Ramayana*.

▼ *Carvings at the nearby temple of Bayon in Angkor Thom shows charging elephants in a battle. This battle, between Cham and Khmer, was lead by King Jayavarman VII*

▼ *Gigantic, serene stone heads are a hallmark of Khmer architecture*

Isn't It Amazing!

Angkor Wat was abandoned in the early 15th century. It was first looted, then left to the mercy of the forests. Experts began to restore it in the 20th century. Today, Angkor Wat is once again an important pilgrimage centre in Southeast Asia. The temple appears on the flag of Cambodia.

▲ *Of the 195 countries of the world, only Cambodia has a building on its flag*

Dynamic Japan

The islands of Japan are prone to earthquakes and volcanic eruptions. Traditional homes in Japan were made to be easily reassembled if they collapsed. Gardens too, play a great part in Japanese architecture. They accompany large homes, temples, and tea houses. The largest buildings were often castles made from timber and sturdy blocks of stone.

▲ Old Japanese buildings of wood were raised off the ground. This Phoenix Hall (Hoo-do) was built in 1053 CE and shows tiled roofs and a Chinese influence

🏛 Tea Ceremonies

The Way of Tea is honoured in Japan with special tea houses (*cha-shitsu*) set in serene gardens. *Cha-shitsu* are usually wooden pavilions with thatched roofs. The walls have large openings that are protected by sliding doors covered with paper. The translucent paper lets in gentle light, setting the atmosphere for drinking tea.

🏛 Shinto Shrines

The Way of the Kami (divine beings) is better known as the religion Shinto. The *torii* is the iconic gateway to Shinto temples. The *kami* lives in the inner shrine, the *honden*. People worship in a hall called the *haiden*. Large shrines have other rooms, such as a hall for ritual dancing (*kaguraden*).

▶ *Choshukaku tea pavilion at the Sankei-en garden. Tea pavilions have no furniture. In fact, no traditional Japanese house does. People usually sit on the floor on cushions or mats*

🏛 Castles

Japan's warrior class built massive fortresses, of which the best preserved is the Himeji Castle. Built strategically on a hill, the castle is guarded by 15-metre-high sloping stone walls. Its 84 small gates limited enemy entrance. Additional protection came from three water-filled moats. Inside, winding passages confused enemy infiltrators. High up in the walls, openings (*ishi-otoshi*) and holes (*ana*) allowed defenders to hurl stones or scalding water, and to fire arrows.

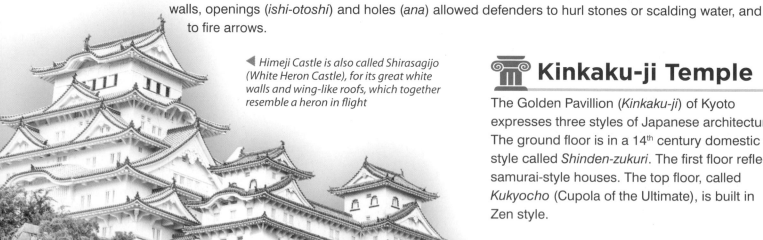

◀ *Himeji Castle is also called Shirasagijo (White Heron Castle), for its great white walls and wing-like roofs, which together resemble a heron in flight*

🏛 Kinkaku-ji Temple

The Golden Pavillion (*Kinkaku-ji*) of Kyoto expresses three styles of Japanese architecture. The ground floor is in a 14th century domestic style called *Shinden-zukuri*. The first floor reflects samurai-style houses. The top floor, called *Kukyocho* (Cupola of the Ultimate), is built in Zen style.

Japanese Gardens

Traditional gardens in Japan mimic nature. They follow simple, harmonious designs. Most gardens were created for relaxation and meditation. Priests in particular studied how to make beautiful gardens. They gave Buddhist names to different parts of their landscape. They even followed Buddhist ideas while designing gardens.

▶ *Spring blossoms on a Japanese cherry tree (sakura)*

Kansho

Gardens built for contemplation are called *kansho*. The entire scenery can be enjoyed by sitting in one place, which is specially constructed for this purpose.

Funasobi and Shuyu

Gardens meant to be explored by boat are called *funasobi*. These were usually built around a large pond. The estate around Byodo-in is laid out in this style. Gardens built especially for strolling are called *shuyu*. The most pleasant sceneries are discovered as you walk along the constructed path. Bridges cross lakes to ensure a continuous walkway.

▲ *Autumn colours at the gardens of Daigo-ji temple, Tokyo*

▲ *Stone pathway across a pond filled with lotus leaves*

▲ *The amazing gardens at the Katsura Imperial Villa combine areas for strolling, boating, and meditation*

Rock Gardens

Both Shinto and Buddhist shrines use sand and gravel to create unique rock gardens. In Zen Buddhism, rock-garden patterns express water and clouds. White sand is used to show purity. Stones are placed to mark islands or mountains in the garden. Altogether, these elements symbolise the beauty and mystery of nature.

Bonsai

An ancient Japanese art, bonsai literally means 'planting in a tray'. It is the method by which dwarf trees are grown. The trees are in fact normal trees, but they are grown in a way that the roots, trunk, branches, and leaves age without growing large. The best bonsai look like mature trees but are small enough to fit in a tray.

◀ *Once the practice of specialists, bonsai trees are even grown by regular people today.*

Pre-Columbian Americas

Before the 16ᵗʰ century, the Americas had thriving and sophisticated civilisations. Their cities and culture were largely destroyed, and later rediscovered by European settlers. The best-known architectural remains belong to the Mayans, Incans, and Aztecs.

Pre-Aztec Teotihuacan

One of the largest and best-preserved Mesoamerican cities is Teotihuacan (The City of the Gods). It holds plazas, temples, palaces, some 2,000 apartments, and even a canal. The broadest road is the 40-metre-wide Avenue of the Dead. At the northern end of the road are amazing stepped pyramids. The largest is the 43-metre-high Pyramid of the Moon. Along the Avenue's southern part is the citadel, a square courtyard that is home to the Temple of Quetzalcoatl, the Feathered Serpent.

▲ *Avenue of the Dead, with the Pyramid of the Moon and lesser stepped pyramids*

Codz-Poop: The Palace of Masks

Mayan architecture has a fascinating variety of elements. The remains of the Palace of Masks show a close matrix of grotesques and masks, in a style called Puuc. The name 'Codz-Poop' means 'rolled blanket'. Though the interiors of the Codz-Poop have not survived the passage of time, the exterior is still impressive. Lots of ruins from the Mayan buildings have simple facades, but Codz-Poop is different. The outside is covered with stones that are shaped like the face of the god of rain.

◀ *The Temple of Warriors at Chichen Itza, Mexico, is one of the few remaining examples of colonnaded (hypostyle) halls in Mayan architecture*

Ancestral Pueblo

Some of the most amazing architecture can be seen in the cliff dwellings of the Ancestral Puebloans of south-western USA. These were most likely built between 1150 CE and 1300 CE. The rooms often had 'doors' on the roof. People climbed up to the roof using ladders, and then came down to the floor through a hole in the ceiling! Each community had two or more *kivas* (ceremonial rooms) that were round, but became square in later times.

◀ *The Ancient Pueblo homes of the Cliff Palace at Mesa Verde National Park in Colorado*

Machu Picchu

Hidden in the Andes mountain range, the ruins of Machu Picchu were once the palace city of the Inca ruler Pachacuti Inca Yupanqui (ruled c. 1438–71 CE). Walking paths and stone steps were carved into mountains which connected ancient plazas, homes, terraces, graveyards, and major buildings. These include the Temple of the Sun and its Military Tower, the temples of the Apollo district, the Princess Palace, and the Palace of the Inca. On three sides, Machu Picchu is bordered by stepped farming terraces, once watered by aqueducts.

Chan Chan, Peru

The largest city in pre-Columbian America was the capital of the Chimu Kingdom (c. 1100–1470 CE), Chan Chan. It was built using adobe brick and finished with mud. The exteriors were often decorated with patterned reliefs and **arabesques**. The city centre held many walled citadels where aristocrats most likely lived. Their cemeteries and storehouses were also in the same area. Each citadel contained pyramidal temples, gardens, water tanks, and symmetrical rooms.

▼ *Machu Picchu is a Peruvian Historical Sanctuary and a UNESCO World Heritage Site. One of the New Seven Wonders of the World*

▲ *Reliefs at Primera Plaza (First Square), Chan Chan*

▲ *Once the largest city in the Americas, the site of the Chan Chan is in ruins today*

Romanesque Architecture

Around the time of King Charlemagne (c. 762–814 CE), Christian basilicas in French areas began to grow larger. These were needed to take in the growing numbers of Christian monks and pilgrims. Larger buildings had to be more thoughtfully constructed, so they would not be crushed by their own weight. Successful new designs began to spread across Europe. Soon, they were applied to other types of buildings. Between the 10th and 11th centuries, these styles developed into what is called Romanesque architecture. It includes formidable masonry (stonework), vaulted ceilings, semicircular arches, unique sculptures, and bell towers.

Aachen Cathedral

The Palatine (royal) Chapel at Aachen Cathedral shows early development of Romanesque architecture. This includes lofty galleries, semicircular arches, and Classical columns.

◀ Charlemagne's Palatine Chapel at Aachen Cathedral, Germany

▲ Built by European crusaders, Krak des Chevaliers is a medieval fortress. Its massive walls and few, small windows are typical of Romanesque castles

▼ The Abbey of Saint-Etienne is a Romanesque monastery founded by William the Conqueror

▶ The Romanesque desire for arcades reached its peak at the Pisa Cathedral. Its famous leaning tower is built with continuous arcading all the way to the top

Ornamental sculpture

Inside, Romanesque churches show masonry with floral and geometrical decorations. Notably, the tympanum—the half-moon space just below an arch—was used to depict figures from the *Bible*.

▲ *Corbels representing the sins of lust, gluttony, and sloth*

▶ *Groin-vaulted colonnade of the cloister at the Old Cathedral of Coimbra, Portugal*

Columns

Romanesque buildings were not only gigantic, they were made of stone (rather than wood). Columns had to bear greater weights. Thus, sturdy drum-like cylinders became popular. Some were even hollow and filled with leftover stone rubble. Alternating columns and piers (load-bearing walls) also helped to distribute the weight.

Vaults

Romanesque buildings were often topped with lofty vaults of stone or brick. The simplest version is the barrel vault—a single arched ceiling that extends from wall to wall. A groin vault is generally square-shaped and built by the intersection of two barrel vaults at right angles. They are often seen in crypts and church aisles.

▶ *A barrel-vaulted ceiling with its original medieval paintings*

Gothic Architecture

Over the 12ᵗʰ and 14ᵗʰ centuries, Christian, and secular styles of Europe came together in the spectacular Gothic style of architecture. This is marked by soaring buildings that reflect a yearning for the heavens. Every part of it, both inside and outside, is crammed with fantastic sculptures, intricate pointed arches, miraculous rib-vaulted ceilings, tall windows, and exquisite stained glass. The truly enormous cathedrals were made possible by an engineering breakthrough called flying buttresses. Altogether, Gothic architecture is an amazing mesh of religion, philosophy, and art.

▲ Gothic sculptures showed a never-before-seen range of iconography. Architects used them liberally both inside and on the facades of buildings

▲ These grim figures with water spouts (often opening out at the mouths) are called gargoyles. They were useful for draining out rain water or channelling fountains

🏛 Flying Buttresses

A buttress is a structure that adds stability to a building. Flying buttresses are made from bars of stone that arch outwards ('fly' out) from the upper walls to a supporting wall (pier). Such buttresses carry the outward pressure placed on walls by heavy roofs. This design allowed the creation of skyrocketing cathedrals, typical of Gothic architecture.

▲ The buttresses at the Notre Dame Cathedral in Paris hold the building up with a deceptively delicate pincer-like hold that is pleasing to the eye

Gothic Arches

Simple pointed windows, called lancets, are a Gothic hallmark. Later Gothic windows show increasing subdivisions of the window (known as mullions) and elaborate tracery.

▶ *Lancet windows at Ripon Cathedral, Yorkshire*

Rayonnant Style

The height of Gothic architecture, Rayonnant is less about size and more about decoration. Architects in the 13th century became bolder with pinnacles, mouldings, and window tracery. Buttresses became more elegant and windows became larger. The topmost walls (between the ceiling and the arches) were entirely replaced with one long, continuous screen of mullioned windows, tracery, and stained glass. These filtered a gentle light into the vast inner spaces, creating an ethereal atmosphere.

Gothic Ceilings

The stability offered by pointed arches and flying buttresses allowed architects to be more creative with vaulted ceilings. New, intricate systems of stone ribs were developed that looked spectacular. They also distributed the weight more evenly between columns and piers, all the way to the ground. Masons were able to make vaults with lighter, thinner stone, so the walls could be opened up to ever-larger windows.

👤 In Real Life

The ethereal beauty inside a Gothic cathedral comes from the soft rainbow light due to its large stained-glass windows. Strange to say, the imperfect glass of the Middle Ages—that is, glass with little bubbles of air trapped in them—is far more brilliant than the smooth, clear glass of modern times. This is because the air bubbles catch and reflect more light and dazzle the eye

▲ *York Minster Rose Window*

◀ *The high Gothic facade of St Vitus Cathedral, with tall mullioned windows and intricate detailing*

ANCIENT & MEDIEVAL ART

AGELESS **ART**

Human beings are social animals. For us, it is essential to express our thoughts and emotions. Art is both a basic and sophisticated form of expression. Even before they invented writing, ancient people were using their fingers and bone fragments, as well as brushes, to scribble down their thoughts in pictures and symbols. Images were also carved into ivory and antlers. These ancient forms of art soon developed in complexity. They extended to other materials, such as paintings on pottery, silk and paper, sculpture, and metalwork. Over the centuries, art has become a part of rituals and ceremonies, an outlet for the imagination, a vehicle for social justice, and even a form of entertainment.

▼ The Moai statues are giant human figures carved from single blocks of stone by the aboriginal people of Easter Island

Prehistoric Art

The earliest examples of human art date from times of myth and mystery. In Africa, Asia, Europe, and South America, art has been discovered from people who lived 40,000 years ago. Such sculptures and paintings are in secluded spots like caves, away from the destructive wind, rain, and new life.

▲ *The Stone Age rock art at Bhimbetka caves shows the earliest signs of human life on the Indian subcontinent*

▲ *The prehistoric site of Stonehenge in England is a famous circle of menhirs (long upright stones). Other such arrangements of ancient human-made blocks of stone can be seen across Europe*

Meaning

Hundreds of prehistoric artworks were sheltered from the open air or hidden away in remote places. These are still around today. They show us what ancient human beings thought, felt, and believed. They show an eternal yearning for beauty, for belonging, and for spiritual meaning.

◀ *In Europe, over the period 30,000–20,000 BCE, female images of all ages were created in abundance. The Venus of Willendorf is the most famous among such figurines*

▲ *This figure of a bison licking an insect bite was carved from the antler of a reindeer between 20,000 and 12,000 BCE in France*

Cave Art

We tend to think of the Stone Age as a time when human societies were basic. But the artworks from this time show us otherwise. In Europe and Africa, the caves where hunter-gatherers lived are covered with paintings, engravings, and low **relief sculptures**. They show hunting packs of humans, fierce animals, and mysterious symbols. Even back then, artists knew to exaggerate certain elements to show a subject's innermost nature. Mammoths and rhinos were drawn with formidable tusks and horns. Horses and deer seemed to move like the wind. Mythical beasts including half-animal, half-human creatures were also created. Portraits of people were rare.

▶ *In the rock paintings of Manda Guéli Cave in Central Africa, camels have been painted over earlier images of cattle. This is perhaps a reflection of the changing climate*

Stone Age Animals

Ancient artworks allow us to see what fearsome and spectacular animals lived during the long Stone Age period. These include the cave lion, ancient bears, the woolly rhinoceros, the sabre-toothed tiger, the mammoth, the giant deer, and the large-horned buffalo. The animals drawn most often were the ones considered useful. In European cave art, for instance, horses, bison, reindeer, aurochs, wild boar, fish, eels, and birds were drawn. They were valued for food, fur, leather, and bone. In Africa, people painted animals in natural combinations like herds of giraffes and elephants, or lakes with hippopotaml, crocodiles, and birds.

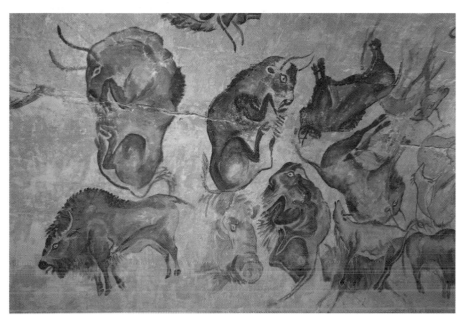
▲ Bisons at Altamira Cave in Spain

 ## Thought and Art

Ideograms are shapes or symbols that convey specific ideas. Prehistoric cave paintings contaln several such symbols. Amazingly, ancient sites from all across the world show many of the same ideas. They show universal human experience and shared concerns, no matter where people lived. For instance, a handprint on a cave wall might have been a person's way of saying, 'I was here'. The symbols also show how ancient human beings were beginning to convey complex thoughts.

Practical Art

When ancient human beings began to settle down, they started drawing pictures of their territories on rocks. These early 'maps' showed cultivated fields, the paths to various houses, and landmarks in the neighbourhood. The Topographical Stone of Jebel Amud, in the Jordanian desert, paints a picture of 150 connected settlements. At the Okladnikov cave in Siberia, human figures have been drawn as well—possibly to show a harvest. An ancient wall map in Turkey shows the settlement near an erupting volcano, the first human record of this phenomenon!

▲ Tin Taghirt in Algeria has exquisite rock carvings; among them is a sleeping antelope and a now extinct buffalo-like animal

▲ Prehistoric handprints decorate the Cuevas de las Manos in Argentina

▲ The Bedolina Map at Valcamonica, a valley in Italy, shows some of the most ancient 'maps'

Mesopotamian Marvels

Mesopotamia is the name given to a vast and ancient land around the rivers Tigris and Euphrates. In modern times, this area covers Iraq and parts of Iran, Turkey, Kuwait, and Syria. Many scholars consider this area to be the birthplace of civilisation. The people who lived in Mesopotamia in ancient times include the Sumerians, Akkadians, Babylonians, and Assyrians. The art of Mesopotamia refers to the art of all these nations. It lasted until Mesopotamia was conquered by the Persian Empire in the 6th century BCE.

Skilled Craftsmen

The most abundant art from Mesopotamia is in the form of pottery and **ceramics**. They were designed with geometric patches and varied in colour. The 6th millennium BCE pottery of Hassuna-Samarra culture shows decorations of human, bird, and animal figures. They are not realistic but stylised figures, emphasising the most attractive features.

In later times, educated people began to use clay reliefs to tell stories. Cylindrical or cubical statues were also developed. Some of the most amazing creations from the 15th century BCE used glass and glazing. The tombs of the rich and the noble at the city of Ur contained beautifully crafted objects of gold, silver, **lapis lazuli**, coloured limestone, and shell. These include jewellery, game-boards, musical harps, weapons, and **seals**.

▲ *This statue of a Sumerian at prayer is made of limestone, alabaster, and shell; it dates back to 2,900–2,600 BCE*

▲ *The Stele of the Vultures narrates the victory of King Eannatum of Lagash over the city Umma, 2,540 BCE*

▶ *Ram in a Thicket is the name given to this stunning figurine found at a site called the Great Death Pit of Ur*

◀ *This is one of 26 Sumerian statues of Gudea, ruler of Lagash, crafted in cylindrical and cubical styles, 2,100 BCE*

▶ *The Standard of Ur, found in the royal tombs, shows peacetime and is made of lapis lazuli and shell*

In Real Life

The earliest known form of nail art dates to ancient Babylonia in around 3,200 BCE. At the time, men coloured their nails to show social hierarchy. Upper-class men wore black nail polish and middle-class men wore green. A solid gold manicure set was discovered in a royal tomb in the city of Ur.

▲ *Babylonian men also curled and set their hair with lacquer*

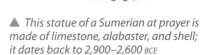

Kudurru

The word *kudurru* is an Akkadian term for a boundary. *Kudurrus* are among the few remaining art pieces marking Kassite rule in Babylonia (16th–12th century BCE). To the Kassite people, these carved boundary stones were a common sight, important both in their economics and religion. The purpose of the *kudurru* was to record the grants of land made by a king to someone who had served him well. The original *kudurru* would remain in a temple. Scribes would copy it on to clay slabs and pass on the copy to the landowner. Apart from the actual grant, engraved gods and symbols festooned the *kudurru*. These apparently brought unholy curses on anyone who dared to go against the king.

▶ *A kudurru of Marduk-apal-iddina II whose name means 'Marduk has given me an heir.' He was an 8th century BCE king of Babylonia who held out against the Assyrian armies for more than a decade*

Wartime Art

In the 10th century BCE, the Assyrians battled and took over their neighbouring lands. They rapidly became the dominant force of Mesopotamia. As is common among victors, they proudly recorded their wars and exploits. They used sturdy limestone slabs, detailed carvings, long inscriptions, colourful bricks, and **frescoes**. Metals were used in the form of imposing gates and sculptures. As the Assyrians won campaign after campaign, they brought home treasures from other nations. The loot included numerous artworks, including bronze vessels, furniture and fittings, ivory carvings, and other technically superb and beautiful works.

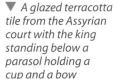

▼ *A glazed terracotta tile from the Assyrian court with the king standing below a parasol holding a cup and a bow*

▲ *An ivory, gold, and lapis lazuli carving of a lion devouring a youth, from Assyrian treasures of 900–700 BCE*

▲ *Religious art from Dur-Sharrukin (Khorsabad, Iraq) from the palace of Sargon II, King of Assyria (c. 722–705 BCE)*

Astounding Egypt

Safe behind its desert borders, ancient Egypt was a thriving civilisation, rich from the fertile land of the Nile. Its wealth and comfort led to the creation of great art forms that served two main purposes. One was spiritual, meant to praise the gods and the Pharaoh, and help people pass into the afterlife. Thus, gods, demons, and mythological beasts were depicted everywhere. The second purpose was to promote Egypt's traditions and values.

▲ *Pharaoh is the title of Egypt's divine ruler, who was worshipped as an avatar of the eagle-headed god Horus, seen in this relief at the temple of Set I*

▲ *The sculpture of Pharaoh Menkaure, with the goddess Hathor and a deity representing the territory of Diospolis Parva*

◀ *A game board bearing inscriptions of Pharaoh Amenhotep III, 1390–1352 BCE*

◀ *The iconic funerary mask of King Tutankhamun*

Crafts and Jewels

Much of the art left behind by ancient Egyptians comes from their amazing tombs. Egyptian pottery was first made from the clay of the Nile and fired to give blackened tops. Later eras used different clays and greater varieties of decorations. Opaque, bright glass was used for amulets, beads, and small vessels. Coppersmiths made small ornaments out of metal. Craftsmen were also skilled in making fine objects from stone. Lavish jewellery came from semi-precious stones, glass, and precious metals. Apart from gold, stones like turquoise, amethyst, jasper, lapis lazuli, agate, and garnet were greatly coveted.

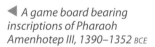

▲ *Winged scarab of Tutankhamun with semi-precious stones*

▶ *Vessel depicting a galloping horse, New Kingdom of ancient Egypt, 18th dynasty, c. 1340 BCE*

Ammut

The demoness Ammut ("the devourer of the dead") had the head of a crocodile, the body of a lion, and the hindquarters of a hippo—all the deadliest man-eaters. She sits by Ma'at (Goddess of Truth), who weighs the hearts of humans on the Scale of Justice. If the heart is as light as a feather, the human is judged to have led a good life. If the heart be heavier, it is devoured by Ammut and the soul is doomed to eternal restlessness!

▲ *Ma'at, Goddess of Truth, wields the Scale of Justice as the crocodile-headed Ammut waits with an open maw*

Faience

Egyptians used a glaze on their pottery made from a ground mineral called quartz. This produced striking blue, green colours and was called *faience*. Faience tiles were used to decorate tombs and palaces. It also produced some of the most amazing jewellery and pottery of the ancient world.

▶ *This faience hippo is one of the finest works from ancient Egypt*

▶ *Lotus-patterned chalice from the 22ⁿᵈ dynasty (945–715 BCE)*

▲ *A faience wall lamp in the shape of a falcon from the Ptolemaic period, 323–30 BCE*

Murals and Paintings

▲ *From the Book of the Dead, the jackal-headed god Anubis brings the scribe Hunefer to judgement. Horus then takes him before the God Osiris, seated before his sisters Isis and Nephthys*

Egyptian murals are abundant in tombs and palaces. In buildings of mud or brick, murals were painted. The themes varied from myths, legends of royalty and nobility, and the daily lives of the people. Entertaining details and hieroglyphs make these paintings compelling. The invention of papyrus gave Egyptian draftsmen another medium to work with. Papyrus paintings flourished and reached a peak in 1300 BCE. This is represented in the *Book of the Dead*, created by the scribe Ani. In later times, pure line drawings became more popular.

Sphinx

With the body of a lion and the head of a human, the sphinx was first seen in Egyptian lore. In Egyptian art, gods were usually portrayed with human bodies and animal heads. The opposite is true for the sphinx, whose face was usually a royal portrait. Sphinxes even wore the *nemes* (headdress) of a Pharaoh. The female sphinx first appeared in the 15ᵗʰ century BCE.

◀ *The most famous and oldest sphinx today is the Great Sphinx at Giza. Arabs call it Abu al-Hawl, the Father of Terror*

Ancient Persia

The land we now call Iran was historically known as Persia. In its prime, the Persian Empire stretched far beyond modern-day Iran. They were wealthy, influential, and amazingly artistic. The earliest artworks from this region are delicate ceramics from c. 3,500 BCE. They belonged to the cities of Susa and Persepolis. Bronze objects from the mountains of Luristan (c. 1,200–750 BCE), and a hoard of gold, silver, and ivory from Ziwiye (c. 700 BCE) are some of the other early artworks of ancient Persia.

▲ Silver cup from the 3rd millennium BCE

▲ A hammered gold ornament from the Ziwiye hoard showing parades of mythical winged beasts

◀ Golden ram-head rhyton (a vessel for drinking)

▲ Pottery from the 4th millennium BCE shows stylised nature, particularly water birds and ibexes (wild goats). They were accompanied by geometrical patterns—a recurring theme in most Persian art

◀ Luristan bronzes were small, flat, amazing objects. They were fashioned as tools, weapons, horse-ornaments, vessels, finials and so forth

▲ Forehead ornament for a horse

▲ Silver bowl with gold decorations from Ziwiye

 ## Achaemenian Art

The first powerful Persian empire lasted from 550 BCE to 330 BCE. Their capital city lay just north of Persepolis. Its most notable kings were Cyrus the Great, Darius the Great and Xerxes I. Artworks from their time show the martial and covetous nature of this empire. Many civilisations were forced to pay tribute. The Achaemenians also established their own coinage and money.

▲ Carved at Persepolis, the famous lion-bull combat is a symbol of Navroz, the Persian New Year. It represents the Earth (bull) and Sun (lion) as being equal during the spring equinox

▲ A panorama at Persepolis shows Armenian people bringing tribute to the Achaemenian king

▲ Gold ornaments show the warrior spirit of the empire

🏛 Oxus Treasure

About 180 pieces of jewellery, statuettes, coins and artefacts of gold and silver make up the fabulous Oxus treasure. No one knows its original owner, but the pieces belong to the Achaemenian Empire.

▲ Winged sphinx at the Palace of Darius in Susa

▲ Ornate gold armlet with griffin heads and a fish-shaped vessel from the Oxus treasure

🏛 Sasanian Art

Persia rose to glory again with the Sasanian Dynasty (220–650 CE). Artists of this empire were skilled in creating decorative stone mosaics, glass, and gold and silver dishes. These were usually ornamented with animals and hunting scenes. Frescoes and illuminated manuscripts also thrived. Crafts such as carpet-making and silk-weaving became a hallmark of Persian art during this period. They were in demand far to the west and east of the world. The most striking remains of Sasanian art are seen in rock sculptures carved on steep cliffs. Famous among these are the sites of Taq-i-Bustan, Shahpur, Naqsh-e Rostam and Naqsh-e Rajab, where the victories of Sasanian rulers are shown. Sasanian artists seem to have influenced the works of Afghanistan (back then a Persian colony), where monasteries bear frescoes and huge Buddhas dating from this period.

▲ The rock art at the Naqsh-e-Rostam depicts the victory of Shahpur I over the two Roman emperors; Valerian and Philip the Arab.

▲ A boar seal of the Sasanian Era, 3rd century CE

▲ Buddhist frescoes at the monastery in Bamiyan, Afghanistan, dating from the 6th century

▲ Amazing silver and gilt vase carved with dancers and flowers

▲ Silver oval cup designed with vines and fruit

Minoa and Mycenae

The Minoans were a trading, seafaring people who lived on the island of Crete (Greece's largest island) during the Bronze Age. Their artists were exposed to ideas and materials from many lands. Their own art depicts a love for nature, particularly sea life. Around 1,400 BCE, they were conquered by armies from mainland Greece. These belonged to the Mycenaeans, who brought a more martial nature to the land. The cultures of both civilisations became one. The art they left behind shows the beliefs and customs of a wealthy, pleasure-loving people.

▲ This 17th century fresco shows seabound Minoans at the town of Akrotiri. In the distance, a lion can be seen chasing stags over the mountains

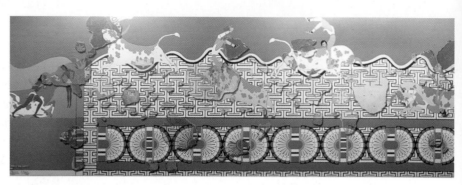

▲ This fresco shows a daredevil Minoan man grappling with a bull

▲ Marching soldiers of Mycenae

▲ The famous Vapheio Cup shows Mycenaeans capturing bulls

◄ The Minoan Snake Goddess

▲ Minoan art drew joyous inspiration from nature, as seen in this intricate gold bee

◄ Ceramic plate from Minoa shows stylised octopuses

🏛 Bull

Minoan art and sport show an affection for bulls. These animals are featured everywhere in Minoan paintings and sculptures. They are often seen with long horns and lithe, graceful bodies, leaping, or combating humans.

▶ Bull head with arching gold leaf horns

◄ Minoan bull leaper

💡 Isn't It Amazing!

Many Greek myths and even the heroic epics of Homer—the *Iliad* and the *Odyssey*—originated in Mycenaean tales.

▲ At the Palace of Knossos, a griffon (part eagle, part lion) graces the throne room

Frescoes

Minoan palaces show true frescoes, called buon frescoes. These are wall paintings where colour is set on wet lime plaster. The colour is absorbed as the plaster dries. This prevents the pigments from fading away over time. *Fresco secco* is the application of colour details on dry plaster. This was used in palaces to give a three-dimensional effect to the art. The paintings were done in red, black, white, yellow, blue, and green. Men were shown with red skin and women with white. Gold was depicted with yellow, silver with blue, and bronze with red.

▶ *Minoan Women*

Jewellery

The smithies of ancient Crete refined metals such as gold, silver, bronze and even gold-plated bronze. Experts made them into jewels, often in combination with semi-precious stones, such as rock-crystal, garnet, lapis lazuli, carnelian, obsidian and jasper. The amethyst from Egypt was popular. Other materials used by jewellers included faience, enamel, soapstone, ivory, shell, and glass-paste. Most jewels were handcrafted. Some, like rings and beads, were made using moulds and casts. Gold was easily the most prized item. It could be beaten, engraved, filigreed, moulded, and punched into exquisite jewellery.

◀ *A rock-crystal **rhyton** from 1500 BCE shows Minoan technique—the neck and body of the vase are joined by a crystal ring decorated with faience; the handle is made from 14 beads of gilt crystal threaded with bronze wire*

▶ *This hefty gold pendant is called Master of Animals. It shows a Minoan God in a field of lotus flowers. He holds a goose in each hand. The whole image is framed by what may be the horns of bulls*

▶ *An ornamental double-headed axe, possibly an offering to a deity*

Pottery

Common forms of Minoan pottery include beaked jugs, *pyxides* (boxes), chalices and *pithoi* (giant storage jars). In later times, these evolved into the more slender floral style. Early Minoan pottery is called *Vasiliki*. It developed into pottery called *Kamares*, which used brightly coloured geometric designs on a black surface. Sea life and human figures were also seen on this pottery. Shells and flowers were sometimes carved onto it. Minoan pottery reached its zenith with the Marine style. This shows a multitude of nature, particularly sea such as octopuses, starfish, shells, sponges, coral, rocks, and seaweed. After the Mycenaean invasions, pottery developed to include the three-handled *amphorae* (a jar for wine and oil), squat *alabastra* (bottles for perfume and massage oils), goblets, and ceremonial vessels with figure-of-eight handles.

◀ *The floral style shows dainty branches, with leaves and papyrus flowers. One of the most celebrated examples is the jug from Phaistos, covered entirely with reed-like decoration*

▶ *Kamares pottery*

▲ *Clay boxes called larnax were used to hold the dead. The larnax show paintings of cattle*

Archaic, Classical, and Hellenistic Greece

Spread around the Mediterranean Sea, ancient Greece was made up of independent city states. However, they shared the same language, religion, festivals, and culture. Most importantly, Greek artists developed their crafts and storytelling skills while Greek tyrants fell from power and one of the world's earliest democracies came to be.

Greek Art

All this is reflected in the incredible art that has influenced the world ever since. Greek artists developed their individual crafts, storytelling abilities and more realistic portrayals of human figures throughout the Archaic Period. The city of Athens witnessed the rise and fall of tyrants and the introduction of democracy by the statesman Kleisthenes in the years 508 and 507 BCE.

◀ The Stag Hunt mosaic from 4th century BCE possibly shows Alexander the Great and his companion Hephaestion

◀ In black-figure pottery, vibrant scenes of black figures were painted on strips of light surfaces and lustrous black backgrounds, as seen in this amphora depicting Achilles and Ajax playing a game during the Trojan War

Pottery

Few ancient Greek works of wood, cloth or painting have survived the wear of time. In contrast, the sturdy fired pottery of Greece is abundant. It shows us the trends and customs of the ancient people. Colourful **mosaic** tiles also give us an idea of what Greek painting might have been like. Pottery vessels were used to store, transport and drink wine and water. Smaller jars were used for perfumes and ointments. In the 8th and 7th centuries BCE, Greek trading brought Eastern influences in pottery painting. Rigid, linear patterns gave way to Asian curvilinear styles and exuberance. Exotic animals like the lion, new motifs, and mythologies began to appear. Perhaps the best known works are the black-figure and red-figure styles of the 7th and 6th centuries BCE. Both focus on dynamic human scenes set in high contrast hues.

◀ The God of grape and wine, Dionysus, in a ship sailing among dolphins; black-figure pottery, 530 BCE

◀ Red-figure pottery was invented in Athens in 530 BCE. It shows light-reddish figures against black backgrounds. This amphora from 440–30 BCE depicts the story of Oedipus and the Sphinx

Sculpture

The best-known figures from archaic Greece are the marble *kouros* (statue of a male youth) and *kore* (statue of a female youth). The style was influenced by Egyptian art like the statue of the Pharaoh with the goddesses. The kouros stands upright with arms at the side and one leg in front of the other. He usually has an elaborate hairstyle. These figures were often used as grave markers. A kore is draped in long fabric and jewellery, and wears a crown. During the Classical Period (480–323 BCE), such rigid sculptures gave way to more natural proportions and postures.

▲ The Kroisos Kouros, in Parian marble, found in Anavyssos (Greece), dating circa 530 BC, now exhibited at the National Archaeological Museum of Athens

▲ The Great Altar of Zeus of Pergamon expresses the agony and drama typical of Hellenistic art

◀ The Hellenistic composition titled Blinding of Polyphemus, a one-eyed Cyclops who was the son of Poseidon, the God of the sea

Art of the Roman Empire

Romans ruled such a large empire for so long that their art reflects styles from many civilisations.
Roman artists imitated and adapted the best trends from the past. They also promoted art and made it available to everyone. They took visual arts to a grand scale—to fit their sense of empire. This triumphant style can be seen in coins, seals, mosaics, frescoes, and, of course, sculpture.

▲ A Roman wall painting depicting the Greek hero Hercules and Omphale, Queen of Lydia

▲ A Roman sestertius (a type of coin) engraved with the betrothal of Marcus Aurelius (who became emperor) and Faustina the Younger (daughter of the then reigning emperor)

◀ The Ludovisi Gaul is a Roman copy of an original Hellenistic Greek sculpture

▲ Ancient bust of Roman Emperor Antoninus Pius (c. 138–161 CE)

▶ The Great Cameo of France is a five-layered piece of jewellery made of sardonyx stone. This Roman artwork dates back to the 1st century CE

🏛 Painting

Inside Roman buildings of all kinds, the walls were richly and beautifully decorated. Bold colours and striking designs were used. They would often cover the wall from floor to ceiling. Designs varied from realistic and ornate subjects to imaginatively stylised works. Themes included human portraits, myths, plants, animals, and even landscapes and townscapes. Skilled artists could create an entire panorama on the walls. From the 1st century BCE onwards, a material called stucco was moulded to create three-dimensional effects and wall reliefs. This was seen in public buildings, homes, temples, tombs, and many other monuments. Painters used natural and deep shades of reds, yellows, and browns, though a number of other colours were also available. For instance, for more plain designs, blue and black pigments were preferred.

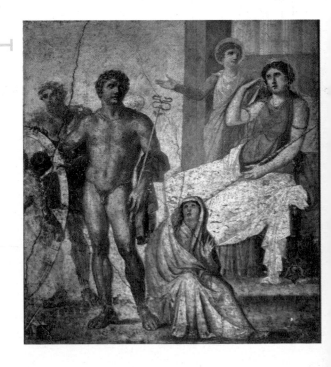

▶ A mural from the 1st century CE villa named House of the Vettii, in Pompeii, shows Juno, the Roman queen of gods, sitting in judgement

Roman Mosaics

A common decoration in homes and public buildings, Roman mosaics were built all across the empire. Mosaic decorated not just floors but also vaults, columns and fountains. They were made using small squares of marble, tile, glass, pottery stone or shells. Black, white and various other colours were used. Popular themes included stories from mythology, heroes, gladiator sports, hunts and nature. As with most Roman art, these often included detailed and realistic portraits of human beings as well. One of the greatest craftsmen of mosaics was Sosus of Pergamom (150–100 BCE) whose works, particularly the *Capitoline Doves* mosaic, was copied many times over for hundreds of years.

▲ A scene from the Iliad where Odysseus (Ulysses) discovers Achilles dressed as a woman and hiding among the princesses at the royal court of Skyros

◀ A mosaic from the House of the Faun, Pompeii, depicts Alexander the Great riding his stallion Bucephalus. They face the Persian king Darius III on his chariot

Sculpture

Roman sculptures can be so true to life, they even show wrinkles, scars and flabby skin! Artists preferred bronze and marble over all other mediums. Roman sculptures combined the clean lines of Classical Greek sculpture with the realism of Eastern art.

Many beautiful Roman pieces are in fact copies of lost Greek originals. In the 1st century CE, Roman sculpture became more adventurous, particularly in creating impressive light and shadow effects. This can be seen in Roman busts, portraits and funerary masks, which often show the truth of the human condition.

▲ Funerary relief of Publius Aiedius Amphio— once a slave, later a free man—and his wife Aiedia, 30 BCE

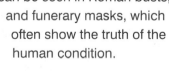

▶ The larger-than-life bronze statue of Emperor Marcus Aurelius on his stallion

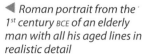

◀ Roman portrait from the 1st century BCE of an elderly man with all his aged lines in realistic detail

Medieval Islam

Islam spread across the world from the 7th century onwards. In medieval times, it influenced Spain, North Africa, Egypt, Central Asia, the Middle East, and the Indian subcontinent, where it developed in unique ways.

◀ Intricate geometric and floral patterns are a hallmark of Islamic art, as seen in this detailing at the Alhambra Palace at Granada, Spain

▶ A circular piece of silk carrying Mongol Il-Khanate images in gold, silk and cotton in early 14th century

▼ Girih is an interlacing design formed from angular lines and standardised shapes, as seen in this 10-point star from medieval Samarkand

▲ A table from the Turkish Ottoman Empire showing patterned tiles on top. The side decorations are a type of inlaid veneer called marquetry

▲ Complex patterns repeat in the details and in the overall designs

🏛 Carpets

Islamic art is closely associated with sumptuous carpets used as prayer mats, wall hangings and floor covers. Warm shades of red and yellow were interwoven with black and cream to give subtle lines and bold effects. These carpets were in great demand across Europe and appear in many Western paintings. Though few carpets have survived from before the 16th century, we can see what they looked like from European paintings. The rugs that have existed till today are considered national treasures.

▲ Detail from the 16th century Mantes Carpet of Persia, depicting animals and hunting scenes

🏛 Carvings

Elaborate carvings were popular in Islam. They were made from the same geometric and floral patterns seen in other forms of Islamic art. Carvings were made from wood, ivory, stone and crystals. They were used to ornament buildings, various types of vessels and even weaponry. Stands for the *Quran*, the Islamic holy book, were carved from wood.

▶ This 10th century ivory pyxis (a medieval jewellery or cosmetic box with a separate lid) comes from Cordoba, Spain. It is carved with fierce scenes from the reign of Caliph Abd al-Rahman III and bears the name of his son Prince Al-Mughira

Painting

Medieval Islam was most famous for miniature paintings in books called illuminated manuscripts. Unlike other forms of Islamic art, miniatures feature human images, even of the Prophet Muhammad. The paintings can be funny, romantic, martial or philosophical. The most famous painters were a part of what is called the Baghdad School of the early 13th century. Miniatures from later periods, as from Mongol Persia, also narrated historical stories.

▲ *Painting of an Arab dhow from 1225–1235*

▲ A 1589 miniature in gold and watercolour shows Babur, the founder of the Mughal Dynasty, receiving a courtier

▲ An elephant clock miniature painting from the *Book of Knowledge of Ingenious Mechanical Devices* by Al-Jazari, 1315

Calligraphy

Decorative writing called calligraphy is seen everywhere in Islamic art. New designs were often created using calligraphy. The content was almost always religious, most frequently about holy names and verses from the *Quran*.

▶ *Calligraphy of the Prophet's name*

▲ *Golden dinars of 11th century Syria with calligraphy*

Mi'raj—The Ascent of Muhammad

A Persian painting of the early 16th century called the *Ascent of Muhammad to Heaven* shows the Prophet's veiled figure surrounded by a halo of flames. This way of partially depicting the holy figure of Muhammad was conventional in the art of the Safavid Dynasty. The painting also shows Chinese influences in the shape of its figures and clouds.

▶ *The 16th century Persian painting shows the veiled Prophet during Isra (the Night Journey), ascending to heaven on the back of a Buraq—a white, winged creature—in the company of angels*

⊕ Incredible Individuals

One of the most skilled calligraphers and Hadith scholars of the 11th century was Fakhr-un-Nisa. Her name means 'Pride of Women'. The daughter of a scholar, she was one of the most knowledgeable people of her era. She was such a charismatic orator that people came from far-flung places to attend her sessions. After the death of her husband, the Caliph granted her a large estate, so she could continue teaching the hundreds of students who came to her. When she died at the age of 90, her funeral was held at Baghdad's Jama'e Al-Qasr and was attended by thousands of people, including scholars, students, and heads of states who mourned her passing.

South Asian Art

There is a long history of beautiful art in South Asia. Bound by mountains in the north and oceans in the south, the area of modern-day Pakistan, India, Bangladesh, Sri Lanka, and parts of Afghanistan form a geographical subcontinent. The people of this area have been united and divided at various points in history. This has led to a kaleidoscope of artistic forms, with shared themes and values. It has been primarily influenced by Hinduism, Buddhism, Jainism, Islam, Christianity, and other more local beliefs.

Indus Valley Art

The Indus Valley Civilisation was a sophisticated Bronze Age culture in what is now Pakistan and northwest India. What we know of their art comes from works of metal and clay works—vessels, figurines, and seals—which give us a clue of what these ancients were like.

▶ The Priest-King statue is carved from soapstone and was found in the Indus Valley city of Mohenjo-Daro (Mound of the Dead)

▶ The Dancing Girl of Mohenjo-Daro

▶ Seals from early Indus Valley settlements showing their hieroglyphic script

Sculpture and Engravings

On the Indian subcontinent, sculpture was the favoured medium for artistic expression. The majority of this art form is inspired by myths and legends of India. Sculptures were also a medium used by empire builders to spread tales of their conquests, and even their laws and beliefs.

◀ A pillar erected by Emperor Ashoka of the Mauryan Dynasty (321–185 BCE)

▲ Some of the finest ancient Indian sculpture comes from the Gupta Empire (319–550 CE). This 5th century piece shows the Hindu god, Krishna fighting the demon horse, Keshi

Mahabalipuram

Fabulous mythological scenes cover the 7th century cave temples by the shore of Mahabalipuram (in southern India). Among them is a relief of the all-powerful goddess Durga riding a lion and slaying the buffalo-headed demon Mahisha.

▲ In a fierce battle, Durga shoots deadly arrows at the fleeing demon, Mahisha

The Greek Influence

Though Alexander the Great was unsuccessful in invading India, Greek styles inspired Indian artists in the north-western areas of the subcontinent. Buddha statues from this time show curly locks and drapery that are hallmarks of Greek statuary.

▶ *The curly locks of the Gandhara Buddha from 1ˢᵗ–2ⁿᵈ century CE are a Greek touch to an Indian figure*

◀ *Engraving of a woman riding a centaur (a creature from Greek mythology) at the Sanchi stupa in central India*

In Real Life

In India, precious and semi-precious stones were thought to have mystical qualities that shielded the wearer against evil forces. Among the most famous of these are the *navaratna* (nine-gem) jewels. *Navaratnas* are worn with the gems in a particular order, even to this day, for the same reason.

◀ *This statue of Lakshmi, the Hindu goddess of wealth, was unearthed in Pompeii, Italy. It is proof of trade between India and Rome in the 1ˢᵗ century CE*

Gold

India's use of gold is as old as the civilisation. In a land that was frequently fractured by the ambition of empire builders and local chiefs, systems of money were always changing. Gold offered a stable source of wealth in unpredictable times. As far back as 5,000 years ago, the Indus Valley was making beads out of the precious metal. The first widely used gold coins belonged to the Gupta dynasty around 250 CE. Since gold is in limited supply, it is frequently melted and recast into newer forms of coins, jewels and precious items. Thus, little original jewellery remains from ancient and medieval times. They can only be seen in the ancient sculptures at Bharhut, Sanchi, and Amaravati and in the paintings at Ajanta Caves. These show that kings, commoners, men, and women, all decorated themselves in a variety of gold ornaments. Indian jewellery is also described in historical literature and in the books and letters of Greek and Portuguese travellers.

◀ *The golden Bimaran casket contains Buddhist relics of the 1ˢᵗ century BCE*

▲ *Kanishka, the greatest king of the Kushan dynasty, was a patron of Buddhism sometime in the late 1ˢᵗ or 2ⁿᵈ century CE. Gold coins from this time show images of Buddha and the king*

Paintings

Given the tropical climate of the subcontinent, few paintings have survived from ancient times. Most of these are on cave walls. The rest are on preserved palm leaves, where they accompany literary works. The subject of such art was religious, martial and imaginative. Some were made to appeal to warriors and rulers. They illustrated legends, romances, and histories.

▶ *Bodhisattva Padmapani from Ajanta Caves, a series of Buddhist rock-cut temples and monasteries created between the 1ˢᵗ century BCE and the 7ᵗʰ century CE*

Imperial China

The art of ancient and medieval China contains some of the most refined and delicate work ever done by humankind. It includes supremely skilled pottery, painting, calligraphy, sculpture, and jade carvings, to name just a few. Much of this art was carefully regulated by successive royal dynasties. Thus, Chinese art forms show familiar motifs that stretch across time and diverse regions.

 ## Ritual Vessels

Shang Dynasty ritual vessels are the earliest remaining Chinese bronze work and include hemispheric pots with three legs called *ding*.

▶ *Ding pots bore mask-like faces and images of tigers, cicadas, owls, rams, and oxen*

◀ *Chinese ritual wine server (guang) from 1100 BCE*

▲ *Terracotta army in the burial chamber of the First Emperor shows the power of royalty in ancient China*

 ▲ *This 26 m long 16th century painting shows the power of the emperor. Called Departure Herald, it shows his luxurious ceremonial procession accompanied by his entourage, their servants, and the accompanying escort of infantry and cavalry*

 ## Painting

Chinese paintings generally used ink made of pine soot and glue. This was dissolved in a little water to get the right consistency. The artist then used a brush made of animal hair, set in finely made shafts of bamboo. Sheets of silk or paper were used for paintings. Fans, albums, vertical hanging scrolls, and horizontal hand-held scrolls (as long as 15 metres) were also painted. Since there was no way to make corrections once the ink touched the sheet, the artists had to know exactly what they were painting, and they would have to execute it with precision. Thus, Chinese artists practised to master speed, confidence, and various other techniques. Paintings were also done on dry plaster walls and screens.

Pigments

Colour was added minimally to give an emphasis but was not essential to painting as it is in other parts of the world. Bright, **opaque** pigments came from minerals—blue from azurite, green from malachite, red from cinnabar or lead, yellow from orpiment or ochre. They were used for silk-based paintings. Translucent vegetable dyes, such as blue from indigo plants, red from safflower, and green from vegetables, were used mainly for painting on paper.

◀ *The 13th century Nymph of the Luo River shows opaque colours used on silk*

Calligraphy

The art of calligraphy has been considered paramount in China since the 3rd century CE. Experts believe it requires great skill and refined judgment. A person's calligraphy is also said to reveal his or her character. In most periods, the calligrapher aimed at depicting rhythm and awareness through the stroke of the brush. Rather than perception or shading, the vitality and composition were considered important.

▲ The teaching of Buddha Sakyamuni, a 12th century painting with abundant calligraphy

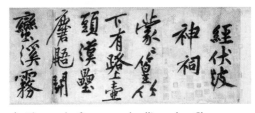

▲ The work of renowned calligrapher Chuang Tching-tiena (1045–1105)

▶ This Wanli period (1573–1620) calligraphy brush is made from badger hair. The pen is decorated with two dragons in silver and gold playing with a pearl

Pottery

As far back as the Stone Age, Chinese artists were producing exquisite painted pottery and black pottery. During the Shang Dynasty (1600–1046 BCE), high-fire stoneware and glazes were invented. During the Han Dynasty (206 BCE 220 CE), a tinted green glaze was developed in northern China. This was used in funerals as it decomposed after burial to give a silvery glow!

Celadon glazes were invented to give ceramics a fine green glaze. Celadon vessels were considered the best for drinking tea. In the 7th and 8th centuries, *sancai* (three-colour) ceramics became popular. They were covered with metallic glazes in green, yellow and brown. The bright colours mixed naturally to produce amazing effects. In the 10th century, fine white ceramics called *ding* were made and decorated with motifs from nature. The Mongol rule inspired blue and white pottery. Later, the Ming dynasty introduced more bold colours producing *wucai* (five-colour) wares.

▶ Painted pottery from the Western Han Dynasty (206 BCE–9 CE) shows raised reliefs of dragons and phoenixes

▼ Chinese sancai wares are the finest ceramics ever made

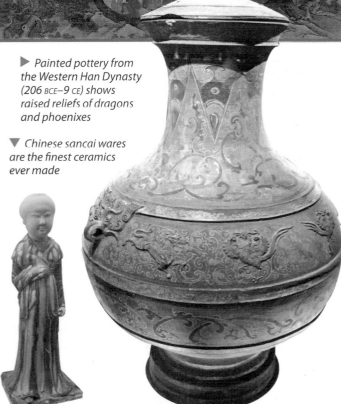

Japanese Art

The earliest form of Japanese art comes from the people of the 10th millennium BCE. However, complex art is generally seen from 7th and 8th century CE onwards. This was also the time when Buddhist influences were seen in Japan. The nation's arts were sustained by imperial and noble families, as well as by shrines and monasteries. Religious art comes from Shinto, Buddhist, and Confucian beliefs. Traditionally, Japanese art is close to nature, whether in showcasing its tranquillity or its drama. The ethics of valour, humility, serenity, and beauty are abiding themes across the centuries. They can be seen in pottery, sculpture, and painting.

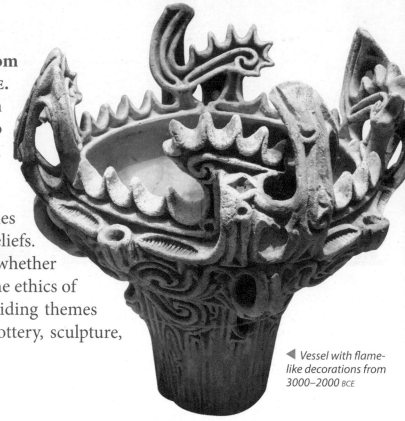

◀ *Vessel with flame-like decorations from 3000–2000 BCE*

Harvest Bells

Bronze bells (*dotaku*) of the Yayoi people were used to pray for good harvests. They were decorated with pest-fighting insects like the dragonfly, spider, and praying mantis.

▲ *A bronze dotaku of the 3rd century*

◀ *A 12th or 13th century statue of a kami, a Shinto god*

Asuka and Nara Art

Between the 6th and 8th centuries, the seat of Japanese government moved first to the Asuka Valley and then to the city of Nara. During this period, Asian influence spread throughout Japan, in particular through Buddhism. As a result, there was an explosion of art forms—particularly sculpture—that incorporated Buddhist legends and local Buddhist tales.

◀ *A bronze dragon-head pitcher patterned with flying horses in gold and silver gilt. A 7th century treasure from the Asuka period*

▼ *The amazing Daibutsu (giant Buddha) at the 8th century Todai-ji temple. Each finger is as large as a person*

Heian Art (794–1185 CE)

The nobility of the capital city Kyoto became devoted to elegant and aesthetic pursuits. The Vajrayana school of Buddhism arrived in Japan. At its centre was the worship of *mandalas*—intricate designs of the spiritual universe. These became a vital part of Japanese art. Paintings such as *raigo* (welcoming approach) were developed. These show the Buddha arriving on a cloud at the time of a person's death.

Bodhisattva

In Japan, the **bodhisattvas** Fugen Bosatsu and Monju Bosatsu are often seen in artworks as Buddha's attendants. Fugen protects devotees of the Lotus Sutra, which offers enlightenment to women. He was worshipped by Heian noblewomen.

▲ *Mandala of the One-Syllable Golden Wheel in the Heian period*

▲ *This hanging silk scroll is a national treasure. It shows the ethereal Juichimen Kannon (Eleven-Faced Goddess of Mercy). Here, Guniyan is represented as a male bodhisattva*

◀ *Sculpture of Monju Busatsu, riding a roaring lion, which symbolises the voice of Buddhist law*

E-maki

Towards the end of the Heian period, horizontal hand-scrolls with paintings became popular. They were called *e-maki*. Two exquisite examples are the 1,130 illustrations of the romantic tale *Genji Monogatari* (Tale of Genji) and the lively 12th century *Ban Dainagon Ekotoba*, a scroll that deals with court intrigues.

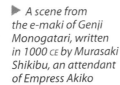

▶ *A scene from the e-maki of Genji Monogatari, written in 1000 CE by Murasaki Shikibu, an attendant of Empress Akiko*

Kamakura Period (1185–1333)

After the 12th century power shifted from the court nobility into the hands of warriors, the arts changed too. It now appealed to martial men. Priests who wished to spread Buddhism also chose art as a suitable medium for the teachings. Realism marked the artworks of the Kamakura period.

Muromachi Period (1338–1573)

Zen Buddhism took root in Japan at this time. Famous monks, priests and legends of Zen were the subjects of early Muromachi art. Paintings were done with quick brush strokes and minimal detail. Later on, a greater sense of space was added to paintings.

▲ *Kamakura period kami artwork at the Shinto shrine Shirayama Hime Jinja*

▶ *A serene Muromachi guardian wearing the armour and helmet of his times*

The Amazing Americas

Before Europeans came to the New World, few American languages had a word for 'art'. People who were skilled with their hands usually worked on weaponry or ceremonial pieces. This is particularly true of the more warrior-like people, such as the Incas and Aztecs. The Mayans had a heavily ritualised religion. Most of their art is focused on pleasing the gods. Thus, art served very specific purposes in the Americas.

▲ From the 8th century, a carving of King T'ah 'ak' Cha'an and two of his people

◀ The Stone of the Sun monolith (single-stone carving) is also called the Aztec calendar stone

▲ A mural of the Jade Goddess (Tlaloc Verde) at the pre-Aztec city of Teotihuacan

Nazca Lines

Geoglyphs are large lines etched into the earth. They are so vast, you can only make out the whole image from a height. The Nazca Lines of Peru are the most famous geoglyphs. They stretch over 500 sq km. Most of these images were created over 2,000 years ago by the Nazca (200 BCE–600 CE), though some are even older. The Nazca Lines generally form images of plants and animals. They include a 285-metre pelican, a 110-metre-long monkey, a 135-metre bird of prey, a 65-metre killer whale, a 50-metre hummingbird, a 46-metre spider, and various flowers and trees. Why they were drawn at all remains a mystery.

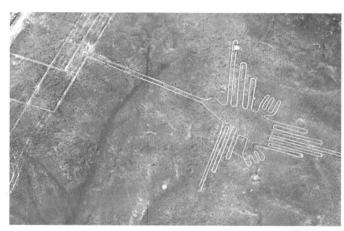

▲ Aerial view of the hummingbird

Metals and Jewels

Gold, silver and copper were the favoured metals of pre-Columbian America. Metalwork from around 4,000 BCE has been found in the Great Lakes region of North America. The earliest gold work, however, is from 1000–500 BCE. It consists of ornaments made from sheets of gold.

By the 16th century, there were well-developed technical skills in fine metalwork in Central America and the Andean regions. Craftsmen would also layer wood, bone, and shell ornaments with gold. They used jade, turquoise, rock crystal, and other precious stones with gold inlays to create exquisite pieces.

⊙ Incredible Individuals

Goldsmiths were so important in the Americas, they had their own patron deities—such as Xipe Totec in Mexico and Chibchachun in Colombia. In Peru, goldsmiths were full-time government employees, working only for the Inca. The craft and all its secrets were carefully guarded, almost like state secrets, and passed on from father to son. ▶ Deity mask of Xipe Totec

🏛 Regional Variation

In Mexico, bimetallic objects—usually with gold and silver—were made by a special casting process. Ecuador made a great leap in metalwork technology when they discovered a way to make complex beads of incredible fineness using an alloy of gold and platinum. It would take Europe another 500–600 years to figure out how to use platinum!

▲ A ceremonial knife of gold, silver, and turquoise, from 900–1100 CE

▲ A Zapotec vampire bat mosaic mask, made of 25 pieces of jade, with yellow eyes of shell

▲ Winged Runner, a Moche ornament from the 3ʳᵈ–7ᵗʰ centuries

▲ This gold serpent—most likely Xiuhcoatl, the deity of fire—is an Aztec lip plug. Its tongue swings from side to side as the wearer walks

🏛 The Tomb of the Lord of Sipan

The Lord of Sipan was an ancient warrior-priest. He ruled the Moche people of Peru during the 3ʳᵈ century. He was 35 or 45 years old when he passed away. The leader was buried with precious ornaments, including a mask and a large, crescent-shaped, feathered headdress. His jewellery includes necklaces, nose rings, earrings, hundreds of shell beads and a gold-and-silver sceptre. The grave also held knives, golden bells and death masks, vessels made of seashells, silver and gold rattles, and golden peanuts (an essential Moche food). A total of 451 treasured objects, and his dog, accompanied the Lord of Sipan to his afterlife.

▲ The tomb of the Lord of Sipan

🏛 Pottery

The American Indians were nomadic people for the longest time. Thus, their pottery culture began at a fairly later stage. Even then, their pottery is unlike anything seen in the rest of the world. One of the main reasons for this is that they did not use a pottery wheel. The clay was moulded or coiled and shaped with hands or on a slow turntable.

◀ A clay vase modelled and painted into a music scene, from the Recuay culture (200 BCE–600 CE) of Peru

◀ Pottery from the Mayan site of Chama shows bold colours and humanised animals

Medieval Europe

The earliest Christian arts of Europe, the Mediterranean, and Russia are called Byzantine. This art flourished from the 4th century onwards. It was influenced by the technical skills, symbols, and styles of Greece, Rome, Egypt, and Persia. During the 9th century, religious art styles began to spread to secular areas. This period is called Romanesque. It was closely followed by Gothic art, which marked the high point of medieval art in Europe.

▲ Gothic frescoes at Elmelunde Church, Denmark

▲ The Miracle of the Child Attacked and Rescued by Blessed Agostino Novello is a painting by the talented Simone Martini (1284–1344), who spread the use of Sienese styles in Gothic art

▲ Made of gilt-bronze, the 12th century Gloucester Candlestick is a testament to Romanesque craftsmanship

▲ From the court of Charles the Bald, Holy Roman Emperor, this plate is made of a coloured stone called serpentine rock. It is inlaid with gold fish and surrounded by 9th century gold and cabochons (deliberately coloured gems)

🏛 Cross-cultural Byzantium

Antioch (in modern-day Turkey) was a large and influential city in Roman times. It helped form the early Christian styles that we call Byzantine art. Located along the Silk Route, Antioch was influenced by the aesthetics of the East. It adopted many oriental motifs, especially from central Asia. The Tree of Life, winged creatures of myth, rams' heads, and full front-facing portraits became common elements. Oriental Byzantine styles spread to the Eastern Orthodox Church. In Russia, it was practised until the 17th century.

🏛 Byzantine Legacy

Paintings and murals formed the bulk of Byzantine art. In particular, artwork in illuminated manuscripts spread Christian symbols across the continents. Embroidery, carvings in ivory, elaborate book covers, gold, and jewels reveal the skills of Byzantine artists and craftsmen.

▶ A pilgrim's flask from Byzantine Egypt showing 3rd century Alexandrian Saint Menas, with camels

▶ Byzantine depiction of the Archangel Michael in gold, enamel, and precious stones at St Mark's Basilica in Venice

▲ The Harbaville Triptych is a Byzantine ivory carving of Christ and the saints

Illuminated Books

In medieval times, books could only be made and copied by hand. Thus, only important subjects such as religion, medicine and governmental affairs were written down. Religious manuscripts, particularly in Islamic and Christian Europe, were decorated with gold or silver, bright colours and small beautiful pictures. These were called illuminated manuscripts. Often, the *Bible's* text was also artfully written with gold and silver ink on pages dyed with Tyrian purple.

▲ *The birth of the Virgin Mary, from an 11th century illuminated manuscript at the Vatican library*

▲ *Illuminated pages of the Homilies of Saint Gregory of Nazianzus, made during 867–86 CE, used Tyrian purple*

Medieval Icons

From the 3rd century onwards, medieval art in Europe was characterised by images of holy figures called icons, these artistic representations were worshipped by Christians. They were most often painted on wooden panels. Colours were mixed with wax and burned into the wood. Some panels were small enough to be portable. Others were used as wall hangings. Icons were also made of mosaic tiles and sculpted into metals, gems, enamel, and ivory.

▲ *The Wilton Diptych is a rare portable 2-panel painting of King Richard II of England kneeling before the icon called the Virgin and Child. Behind him stand three saints, two of whom were previous kings of England*

In Real Life

Refined tableware of gold, silver, china and glass has been attractive to people ever since they were first invented. In Byzantine times, large numbers of silver plates were stamped with Christian images and used for dinner service.

▶ *A 7th century dinner plate from Constantinople with stories of David from the Bible*

Mosaics

Since Byzantine times, mosaics were used extensively to decorate walls and ceilings. Most medieval European mosaics depict religious figures. Gold tiles were a favourite, since they gave a shimmery effect. This reinforced the feeling of being in the presence of heaven. Occasionally, pagan gods, mythical beasts, and scenes from royal life would find their way into the art.

▲ *The 13th century mosaic by Jacopo Torriti shows the coronation of the Virgin with angels, saints, Pope Nicolas IV, and Cardinal Colonna. Parts of the mosaic belong to the original 5th century work*

▲ *Floor mosaic of African animals being hunted and herded found in the early Byzantine church at Mount Nebo (Memorial Church of Moses) built to commemorate the place where Moses passed away*

Masterpieces of the Dark Ages

The early centuries of the medieval period are often called the Dark Ages. At this time, art was made for high-ranking priests and lords. Much of the actual work was done by monks. They were untrained men whose efforts were rarely acknowledged. Even though they created a whole new movement of art, the artists remain a mystery.

 ## Roman Catacombs

A catacomb is a large underground cemetery where people were buried in medieval times. The Roman catacombs are decorated with some of the earliest Christian art. The paintings and mosaics here are simple. Some of them tell stories and some are symbolic. The tales express the human yearning for eternal life; to be free of death. There is the story of Lazarus who was raised from the dead by Christ, four days after his body was entombed. The tales come from both the *Old Testament* and *the New Testament*.

▶ *The Virgin and Child fresco at the Commodilla Catacomb of Rome*

 ## Symbolic Art in the Catacombs

Many Christian ideas and beliefs are painted on the catacomb walls. The sign of heaven's peace is a dove. To show immovable faith, an anchor is drawn. On the slabs of the graves, more personal symbols can be seen. For instance, an engraved tool shows you what that person's job used to be. Many symbols refer to salvation, heaven and a new life. These include the peacock, the lamb and the phoenix.

◀ *The members of a family are painted above their tomb with their hands raised in prayer. The crown above the girl's head symbolises victory over death*

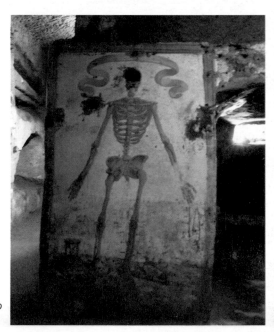

▶ *The painting of the skeleton (representing death) with an hourglass and a crown by its feet shows how death comes to all in time—even to kings*

Bayeux Tapestry

The current Queen of England can trace her family all the way back to 1066, when Duke William of Normandy (in France) conquered England and made himself king. The story of this conquest is told in the amazing Bayeux Tapestry. This embroidered cloth is over 70 metres long. The tapestry is like a movie, with heroes, plots, action, romance, and battles. It has armies, animals, kings, knights, fortresses, ships, and many other elements. Experts think the Bishop of Odo—William's half-brother—paid for the tapestry to be created in the 1070s.

◀ *Bishop Odo rallies the troops in battle, embroidery from the Bayeux Tapestry*

Isn't It Amazing!

Early Christians believed that a peacock's flesh did not decay after death. Thus, they used the peacock as a sign of immortality.

In Real Life

Nowadays, artworks can fetch their creators thousands, even millions, of dollars. But during the Dark Ages, artist-monks received almost nothing. In contrast, the Church or State spent lavishly on the art itself. Gold (in the form of dust, foil or leaf), silver, rare gems, expensive colours and fine calf-skin canvasses were used to create masterpieces that can be admired even today.

The Apocalypse of Beatus

Beatus was an **abbot** of Libeana (in northern Spain). Around 776 CE, he wrote a masterful account of the Apocalypse—the Biblical end of the world—with multi-headed beasts, trumpeting angels and horrifically punished sinners. His *Commentary on the Apocalypse* became so popular that many monasteries made a copy of it. This was in the days when books were copied by hand. Today, 25 copies of Beatus' book exist. These were made between the 10th and 13th centuries. They vary from large and gloriously illuminated works meant for cathedrals to smaller editions for personal use.

▲ *The Sixth Seal by Spanish painter Magius*

▲ *The Dragon Gives His Power to the Beast, from the Beatus de Facundus (1047)*

▼ *Scenes from the early section of the Bayeux Tapestry*

MODERN
ARCHITECTURE

MOVING TOWARDS MODERNITY

From the 16th century onwards, exploration and empire-building brought new ideas and greater wealth to Europe. This gradually gave rise to an age where religious zeal was tempered by reason and science. One of the most remarkable gifts of advancing technology was its impact on architecture. Engineers and architects were able to look at new forms of construction that were previously unavailable to them. Sometimes it was because new solutions in mathematics and engineering came into being. Sometimes it was because of innovations in processing. Sometimes it was because they found new ways of using materials like iron, concrete, and steel. The plethora of choices combined with the unending imagination of architects gave rise to this brilliant new pre-modern era of architecture.

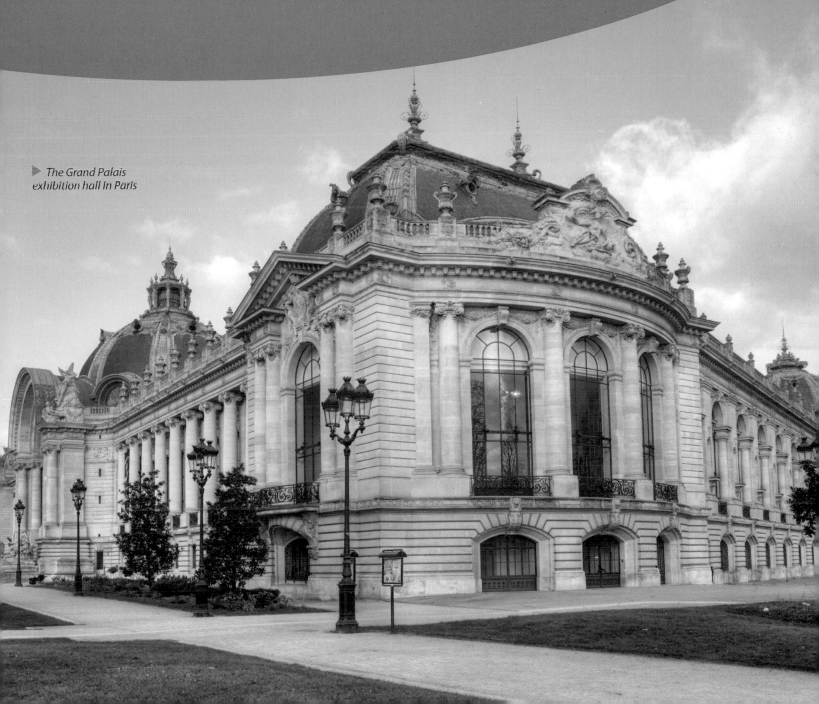
▶ *The Grand Palais exhibition hall In Paris*

Baroque Grandeur

In the late 16th century, Italian architects set aside the strictly proportional designs of the Renaissance era. Their compositions became more complex, detailed and sensual. This marked the start of the Baroque period, a time of grandiose and dramatic architecture that influenced buildings all across the West. In some places, like Germany and South America, it lasted until the 18th century.

▲ The amazing, illusory frescoes seen under the dome of the Church of Gesù in Rome were created by Baroque artist Giovanni Battista Gaulli (also called 'Baciccio')

▲ St Paul's Cathedral is a masterpiece of English Baroque architecture created by astronomer, mathematician and one of England's most influential architects, Christopher Wren (1632–1723)

Counter-Reformation

In the 16th century, many Christians had lost faith in the Catholic Church. A number of reformers came forth to change its practices, to remove its decadent and wrongful ways. Many of these reformers believed that art was a sin. But the Catholic Church knew how important art and architecture were to ordinary people. They understood that Christians needed holy places and divine paintings to feel close to God. Thus, they planned the Counter-Reformation movement. A key part of this plan was to use grand and powerful art and architecture to win back the people. The Baroque constructions were the result of Counter-Reformation.

▲ Lying between curved, colonnaded arms, the vast Baroque square of St. Peter's Cathedral can hold thousands of people in its embrace. This is a symbol of the Catholic Church welcoming its faithful to the fold

Baroque Styles

In keeping with the Catholic Church's wish to appeal to people's senses, baroque architecture was made to be vivid and fantastic. Architects built complex and palatial structures with richly embellished surfaces. Interiors were marked with twists and turns, dazzling displays of light, bright colours and sharp contrasts. Curved, gilded statues entwined with each other in weird and wonderful compositions. Walls and ceiling were covered with hypnotic, illusory paintings. Such imaginative grandeur had never before been seen. It was as much admired as criticised. 'Baroque' is sometimes used to mean extravagant, deformed and even absurd.

▶ *Adorning St. Michael's Church in Vienna is The Fall of the Angels (1781), a fabulous stucco relief sculpted by Austrian talent, Karl Georg Merville*

Palace of Versailles

Baroque architecture flowered into its most opulent forms in France. Nowhere is this more clearly visible than the spectacular Palace of Versailles built by Louis XIV (1638–1715), the Sun King. His royal residence was the combined effort of many brilliant men, including his favourite architect, Jules Hardouin-Mansart.

The palace's designs were typically Baroque in that their focus point was the interior, specifically the king's bedroom. From there, a series of divisions and repetitive motifs formed an awe-inspiring complex of buildings. This included two other palaces, the Grand Trianon and the Petit Trianon. Its symmetrical gardens, with their fountains of dragons, lions, nymphs and gods, were designed by the most influential landscape architect in French history, André Le Nôtre.

◀ *The king's bedchamber at the Palace of Versailles*

👤 In Real Life

The most famous room in the Palace of Versailles is the Hall of Mirrors. Built over 1678–1689, this 70-metre-long gallery is lined with a series of large mirrors opposite equally large windows. Delicate glass chandeliers hang down from the arched, richly painted ceiling. Gilded statues and decorations cover the gallery. The entire effect is one of dazzling light and splendour.

▶ *The Hall of Mirrors*

Baroque in Habsburg Lands

For centuries, the House of Habsburg controlled Spain, Austria, Hungary, parts of the Netherlands, and many overseas colonies. At the time of Reformation, Charles V was the king of all these territories. He was also the Holy Roman Emperor, which made him a Catholic ally and supporter of the Counter-Reformation movement. Charles V's heirs continued in his footsteps and the Baroque period flourished throughout the Habsburg Empire.

▲ Designed by German architect Andreas Schluter and Danish amber craftsman Gottfried Wolfram, the Amber Room at Berlin City Palace was called the 'Eighth Wonder of the World'. Unfortunately, it did not survive WWII

▲ Located in the Grand Square of Sibiu, Brukenthal Palace (1777–1787) was the official home of the Habsburg Governor of Transylvania, Samuel von Brukenthal. In 1817, it became (and remains) one of the earliest museums in the world

 ## Spain

Baroque styles from Italy began influencing Spain in the 17th century. Around 1667, talented men like Alonso Cano and Eufrasio Lopez de Rojas began adding Baroque-inspired motifs to the exteriors of Granada Cathedral and the Cathedral of Jaen, respectively. The celebrated Churriguera family of architects were most influential during the late 17th and early 18th centuries. Their name is synonymous with Spanish late-Baroque architecture. The intricate and exaggerated Churrigueresque style was later introduced to Mexico— a landmark structure being the Cathedral of Zacatecas— and to the Philippines.

▲ Churrigueresque grandeur at Granada Charterhouse's inner sanctuary

⊙ Incredible Individuals

Painter, sculptor, and architect Alonso Cano (1601–1667) produced religious works of such evocative strength, that he was dubbed the Spanish Michelangelo. Cano led a tumultuous life. In 1638, he fled Seville after a duel with an artist. In 1644, he escaped again when he was suspected of murdering his wife. Cano later took holy orders and became the chief architect of Granada Cathedral until his death.

▲ Granada Cathedral's Baroque facade was designed by Alonso Cano

Hungary

Built by Pietro Spozzo over 1629–1637, the Jesuit Church of Nagyszombat is perhaps the first great Baroque building in Hungary. During the 17th and 18th centuries, Jesuit patrons used the Baroque style to rebuild areas conquered from the **Ottoman Empire**. This included townscapes of places like Gyor (1630s), Kosice (1670s), Eger (1730s) and Szekesfehervar (1740s). The Royal Palace in Buda, Grassalkovich Castle in Godollo, and Esterhazy Castle in Fertod are the nation's most important Baroque structures.

▲ *Buda Castle, the massive home of Hungarian kings, rises from the banks of the River Danube and towers over the city*

The Low Countries

Joining the spirit of the Counter-Reformation movement, the Catholic churches in the southern region of the Low Countries set up many important architectural projects. Perhaps the most famous Flemish architect of this period is Wenzel Coebergher. He trained in Italy and is best-known for the heptagonal (seven-sided) Basilica of Our Fair Lady of Scherpenheuvel.

◀ *Spanish, French, and Dutch Baroque aesthetics come together in the Abbey of Averbode (1667) in Belgium*

In Real Life

The Marian cult of Scherpenheuvel began when the villagers of Zichem flocked to worship a statue of the Virgin Mary on an oak tree upon a hill. The shrine took on its beautiful Baroque shape under the patronage of the Habsburg rulers Ferdinand and Isabella. It is said to be the most popular pilgrimage site in Belgium.

The Holy Roman Empire

In the early days, master masons from Italy and Switzerland dominated the baroque scene. Over the 17th century, Austria developed its own style. The Austrian architect Johann Fischer von Erlach combined elements of Classical and Baroque styles, forming a new style popular with the Imperial power. After him, military engineer Johann Lucas von Hildebrandt became the leading court architect. The empire also adopted French palace architecture, particularly, the horseshoe-like layout, enclosing a courtyard on the town side. The outstanding German palace of this period was the Würzburg Residence. It blends Austro-Italian and French designs.

▼ *Baroque glamour in Germany's spectacular Würzburg Residence*

Baroque in Eastern Europe

The German-Baroque touch spread to Poland, the Baltic States, and Russia. The early Russian style, seen at the end of the 17th century, is called Naryshkin Baroque. It is marked by elegant white ornamentation on red-brick walls, usually at churches. The style changed under Dutch influence into Petrine Baroque. It was named after the nation's powerful monarch, Peter the Great. The period culminated in the opulent Rastrelli style. Named after architect Bartolomeo Francesco Rastrelli, this style combined elements of Rococo with Russian aesthetics to produce amazing, multicoloured structures. Favoured by the Russian empresses Anna I and Elizabeth I, Rastrelli erected numerous palaces for members of the imperial court for over 50 years.

▲ Naryshkin Baroque was originally seen in the Church of the Intercession of the Virgin at Fili (1693), on the estate of the boyar Naryshkin

▲ This painting by Konstantin Ukhtomsky shows the Jordan Staircase, one of Rastrelli's 18th century masterpieces at the sumptuous Winter Palace

🏛 Petrine Russia

Tsar Peter the Great (1672–1725) inherited a love for art and architecture from both sides of his family, Naryshkin and Romanov. When he came to power, he dedicated a lot of time and resources to building St. Petersburg into a grand centre for culture and scholarship. Every building erected there had to first meet his design approval, in particular, his palaces and gardens that were constructed by the sea. Most buildings at this time were made with brick or stone to lower the risk of fire. This gave rise to a city that embodied a new Russian expression of scale, colour, and form. It rapidly spread to other parts of the country, where it developed regional variations. Unfortunately, much of this Petrine Baroque architecture was destroyed during the 20th century.

⭐ Incredible Individuals

Rastrelli's style attracted so many followers, it led to a distinct school of architecture. In 1749, Prince Dmitry Ukhtomsky (1717–1774), a student of Rastrelli's, established one of the earliest Russian architectural colleges in Moscow.

▲ Rastrelli's spectacular ballroom in Catherine Palace

◄ Located on the Neva riverfront, the turreted Kunstkamera is Russia's first museum. Established by Peter the Great, the building was designed by German architect Georg Johann Mattarnovy and constructed over 1719–1727

Peterhof Palace

After a visit to the French court in 1717, Peter the Great commissioned the Peterhof Palace to rival the royal residence at Versailles. The largest of its palaces, the Grand Palace, was designed by Domenico Trezzini from 1714–1728. The gardens were planned by Alexandre Le Blond. In 1752, Bartolomeo Rastrelli made the palace even larger, thus making it the most opulent summer residence of the Russian royalty.

▲ *Exquisite statues of gold adorn the steps and the grand cascade of fountains in front of Peterhof Palace*

The Polish-Lithuanian Commonwealth

The Kingdom of Poland and the Grand Duchy of Lithuania were ruled by a single Catholic monarch. Thus, both nations were early adopters of Counter-Reformation and the Baroque forms. The commonwealth's oldest Baroque church is the 1587 Corpus Christi Church in Nesvizh, Belarus. It also has the oldest domed basilica with a Baroque exterior. This period was influenced by Eastern, specifically Ottoman, ideals. The German architect Johann Christoph Glaubitz (1700–1767) developed a distinct and popular Vilnius Baroque style, best seen today in the old town of Vilnius.

Towards the end of the century, the influence of Polish Baroque could be seen in the **Cossack Hetmanate**. Here, the style is combined with Orthodox architecture to give rise to the unique and popular Ukrainian Baroque style of architecture.

▲ *The 18th century Visitation of Our Lady Basilica at Wambierzyce, a beloved pilgrimage site in Poland*

Christoph Dientzenhofer

The Bavarian architect Christoph Dientzenhofer (1655–1722) was a leading architect of the Bohemian Baroque style. He transformed Prague and Bohemia with his boldly designed buildings.

▶ *Built by Dientzenhofer and his talented son, Brevnov Monastery is a flowing structure of curved walls and intersecting oval spaces*

Resplendent Rococo

In France, high Baroque aesthetic was combined with a delicate, decorative form of art and architecture to produce Rococo. This style came into being after the death of Louis XIV and flourished until the French Revolution. Though primarily associated with France, it spread to other parts of Europe for a short time. Rococo is more light and charming than the grand and ponderous Baroque. Where Baroque architects designed horizontally separate structures, Rococo architects created unified spaces. This allowed them to produce continuous themes in decoration.

▲ *Delicate 18th century decorations on the walls of the French prime minister's office at Hotel Matignon*

▲ *The Hall of Mirrors at Amalienburg is a grandiose 18th century hunting lodge in southern Germany*

Louis XV Period

Rococo opulence is sometimes seen as a symbol of the decadence that existed in the years before the French Revolution. It reached its peak during the long reign of Louis XV (r. 1715–1774). For this reason, interior designs and furniture pieces from this time are said to belong to the 'Louis XV period'. Unlike the Catholic Baroque, Rococo took place in an age of growing secularism. It was aimed at pleasing the senses using asymmetric, often **arabesque** schemes. The style was pioneered and developed by interior designers, artists and craftsmen such as Nicolas Pineau (1684–1754), Juste-Aurele Meissonnier (c. 1693–1750) and Pierre Le Pautre (1659–1744). The fashionable interiors of the Chateau de Chantilly (c. 1722) and Hotel de Soubise in Paris (c. 1732) mark the high point of the Louis XV period.

▲ *The ceiling of the Salon de la Princesse in Hotel de Soubise, Paris*

Isn't It Amazing!

The castle in the Disney movie *Beauty and the Beast* was inspired by Rococo. Lumiere, the enchanted candlestick, bears a striking resemblance to the works of J. A. Meissonnier, in particular the goldsmith's iconic candelabra from around 1735.

▶ *Meissonnier's famous silver candlestick resembles twists of leaves and flowers*

Rococo Affectations

Lavish Rococo combined two styles—the French Rocaille, a delicate, symmetrical form of decoration inspired by nature, and the heavy Italian Barocco (Baroque). The French word *rocaille* refers to shells, rocks, and similar-shaped knick-knacks that adorned grottoes and bordered fountains. Other common themes included fish, birds, bees, climbers, leaves, and flowers. The homes of the well-to-do were cluttered with clocks, frames, mirrors, candlesticks, and furniture that employed this form of ornamentation. Decorative statuary and paintings were thus an integral part of Rococo architecture.

Chinoiserie

First appearing in the 17th century, *chinoiserie* is the interpretation of Chinese motifs in Western art. Stylised dragons and phoenixes were popular during the Rococo period. Structures like the Chinese House in Potsdam, Germany and the Chinese Village in Tsarskoye Selo, Russia, were built in a mix of Rococo and *chinoiserie* style.

▲ The Rocaille wall clock (c. 1745–1750) is shaped like a shell. It is the work of watchmaker Ferdinand Berthoud and sculptor Jacques Caffieri

▲ Porcelain from Vincennes, France depicting a Chinese rural scene

◀ Designed by Johann Gottfried Buring, the Chinese House was built by Fredrick II of Prussia in a garden of his summer palace. It served as a teahouse

Rococo in Europe

Rococo architecture became immensely popular in Eastern Europe and Russia. Western Europe more easily accepted its interior fashions. The abbey church, built by the Asam brothers in Weltenburg, Germany, is typically theatrical with its oval simplicity offset by rich white-and-gold ornamentation. Beyond the high altar is an amazing sculpture of St. George spearing a writhing dragon. Flemish architect Jaime Borty Milia introduced Rococo to Spain when he constructed the west facade of the Cathedral of Murcia in 1733. Spanish Rococo found its greatest champion in Ventura Rodríguez, who created the dazzling interiors of the Basilica of Our Lady of the Pillar in Saragossa (1750).

▲ Welternburg Abbey's Rococo interior with its famous sculpture of St. George and the dragon

◀ The extraordinary hanging sculpture at the high altar of the former monastery Rohr, in Germany, was created by Egid Quirin Asam (1692–1750)

Neoclassical Architecture

Classical architecture refers to ancient Greek and Roman constructions. The style was revived and further developed during the Renaissance period between the 14th and 16th centuries. When it flourished again during 1750–1830, it was described as the 'true style'. In later days, it came to be known as Neoclassicism. At this time, people were exploring, digging, and discovering Classical sites in Italy, Greece, and Asia Minor. This naturally led to a renewed interest in Classical studies, which coincided with the European **Age of Reason**. The movement was marked by a search for architectural truth. It rose against the illusion, ornament, and exaggeration of the Baroque and Rococo eras.

▲ The Konzerthaus (concert hall) on Gendarmenmarkt square is one of many architectural gems designed for Berlin by city planner Karl Friedrich Schinkel (1781–1841)

▲ Tired of Rastrelli excesses, Queen Catherine the Great (c. 1762–1796) of Russia summoned Scottish architect Charles Cameron (1745–1812) to build the Neoclassical Pavlovsk Palace in Saint Petersburg

▼ The Pantheon in Paris is an early Neoclassical landmark designed by Jacques-Germain Soufflot (1713–1780), who studied the ruins of ancient Rome

🏛 The Pioneers

Neoclassicism rose in England and France. The writings of **Hellenist** art historian Johann Joachim Winckelmann inspired a generation of architects to explore Neoclassicism. This expressed itself in the Louis XVI style in France, where Classicism-inspired motifs were used to decorate buildings. This evolved into a more austere style called Directoire. It was pioneered by men such as Charles Percier (1764–1838) and Pierre-Francois-Leonard Fontaine (1762–1853). During the reign of Napoleon Bonaparte, Neoclassicism developed richer, more imperial tones. This phase is named Empire style.

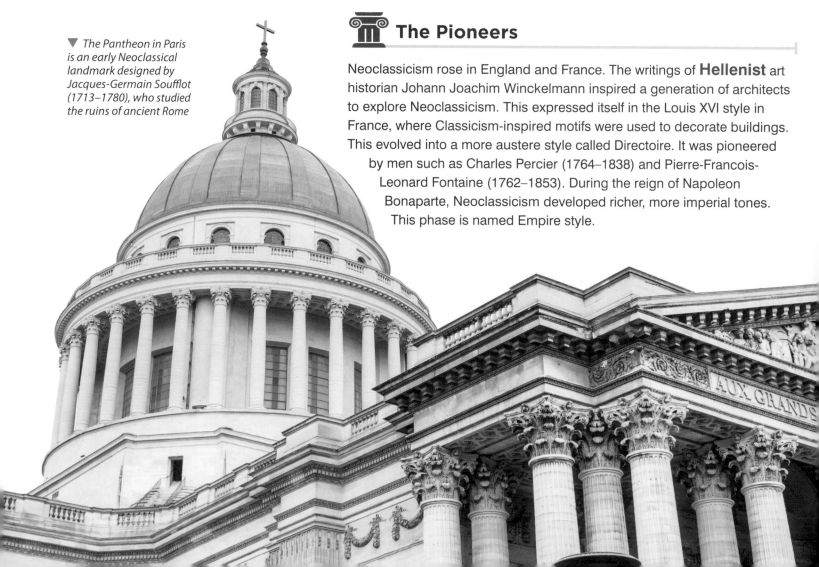

Neoclassicism in Britain

The British Isles used imposing Neoclassical designs to construct public buildings such as banks, museums, and post offices. Notably, John Soane (1753–1837) designed the Bank of England and Robert Smirke (1780–1867) created the British Museum, the General Post Office, and Covent Garden Theatre. Possibly the most famous architect of this time was John Nash (1752–1835). His designs for parks and city blocks changed the appearance of London. Among his creations are Regent's Park, Carlton House Terrace, and the Buckingham Palace.

▲ The Neoclassical facade and palatial extension of Buckingham House was commissioned by King George IV (1762–1830) and designed by John Nash

Incredible Individuals

The Arc de Triomphe in Paris was commissioned by Napoleon Bonaparte in 1806 to commemorate his victory in Austerlitz. Based on ancient Roman arches, this ostentatious structure was finished only in 1836, 25 years after the death of its architect, Jean Chalgrin.

▲ The world's largest freestanding triumphal arch, the Arc de Triomphe, Paris

Palladianism

Andrea Palladio (1508–1580) was one of the greatest architects during the late Renaissance period. His theories of rationality, order, and symmetry in buildings heavily influenced Neoclassical architects. The resulting movement was called Palladianism. The first Palladian house of the 18th century was Wilbury House, built in Wiltshire by William Benson, a member of Parliament. Champions of the style included the Scottish architect and publisher Colen Campbell (1676–1729), Richard Boyle, third Earl of Burlington (1694–1753), and his protégé William Kent (c. 1685–1748).

▲ Burlington's home, Chiswick House, was inspired by Palladio's famous Villa Rotunda

▲ One of Colen Campbell's impeccable Palladian creations, Houghton Hall in Norfolk was commissioned by Robert Walpole, who is regarded as Great Britain's first prime minister

▲ In 1769, George Dance the Younger modified London's Newgate Prison along Palladian lines. The imaginative new building had grim drama and was one of the city's most original constructions until it was demolished in 1902

Classicism in the New World

Neoclassical architecture found its true home in the Americas. A notable early architect of the style was the third president of the USA, Thomas Jefferson (1743–1826). He famously created the Virginia State Capitol and his own home, Monticello ("little mountain"). During the 19th century, the newly formed USA built many public buildings, even universities, in the Neoclassical style. In Latin America too, military engineers and urban architects built imposing public structures such as hospitals, prisons, banks, and post offices. As a result, many nations of the New World closely identify with Classical aesthetics.

▲ In 1844, a fire swept through the Cathedral of Arequipa in Peru. Architect Lucas Poblete rebuilt and expanded the cathedral into a unique structure, incorporating the triumphal arch motif from Classical canons

▲ The symmetrical and refined La Moneda Palace in Santiago is the seat of the president of Chile. It was built around a series of vast courtyards in the late 18th century by architect Joaquin Toesca y Ricci

🏛 The Federal Style

The Classical theories of ancient Rome resonated with the ideals of the new US republic. Neoclassical designs seen in this young nation, especially over 1785–1815, are called Federalist. The style originated with the works of Jefferson, Benjamin Latrobe (1764–1820), and Charles Bulfinch (1763–1844). The architecture is marked by plain and austere surfaces. It carries Classical motifs like panels, tablets, and friezes. The ruins of ancient Roman towns around Mount Vesuvius, such as Pompeii and Herculaneum, deeply influenced Federalist styles.

▲ Elfreth's Alley is a historical street in Philadelphia. It is famous for its Federalist-style homes, built over the 18th century for shipwrights, furniture craftsmen, glass-blowers, silversmiths, and other tradespeople

👤 In Real Life

Designed by Jefferson, the Virginia State Capitol is the first public building in the US to be modelled entirely on a Roman temple, specifically the 1st century Maison Carrée in southern France. Designed in partnership with Charles-Louis Clérisseau (1721–1820), the stucco-clad brick building took almost two decades to build and was further added to during the 19th century.

▲ This 1865 photo shows the Capitol building in Richmond, Virginia, in Jefferson's original design, before it was renovated and expanded

Massachusetts State House

A landmark building designed by Bulfinch is the Massachusetts State House (1795–1797). It was inspired by London's Somerset House, an amazing Neoclassical mansion created by Scottish-Swedish architect William Chambers. The Massachusetts State House is remarkable for its main dome. This central feature was so well-liked, it became a standard part of most other state-capitol designs.

▲ The famous wooden dome of the Massachusetts State House was gilded at great expense during the late 1990s

 ## The Egyptian Obsession

American Neoclassicism was also fascinated and influenced by ancient Egypt. Between 1848–1888, America built the colossal obelisk—a structure from ancient Egypt and Rome—called the Washington Monument. It was also the tallest structure in the world until the Eiffel Tower was built. At just over 169 metres, it remains the tallest structure made of stone and the tallest obelisk in the world.

◀ Sunrise over the Egypt-inspired Washington Monument, located beside the Greek-inspired Lincoln Memorial, with the Rome-inspired Capitol Building in the distance

 ## Capitol Building, Washington, D.C.

The US Capitol Building was designed by the physician Dr William Thornton (1759–1828). His plan showed a grand entrance with projecting horizontal wings. The central building rose on vertical columns and was crowned by a magnificent dome. Some of these structures were built out of wood and later rebuilt using stone and iron. Since Thornton was not an architect, a number of more formally trained men oversaw the actual construction. This included Benjamin Latrobe and Charles Bulfinch, who added their own designs to Thornton's plans. The cornerstone was laid by President Washington on 18 September 1793. Construction continued well into the 19th century, while much renovation and modernisation took place in the 20th century. Today, the awe-inspiring Neoclassical facade and dome of the Capitol are among the most recognisable American icons.

▲ The eastern facade of the US Capitol Building, Washington, D.C., with its spectacular central dome

Romanticism in Architecture

During the 19th century, Europe was wealthy and changing rapidly. New territories were being conquered overseas, and through the returning ships, new influences swept into the continent. While the exotic was eagerly adopted, Europe eventually became nostalgic for its older, home-grown styles. The resulting architectural revival was marked by a romantic remembrance of those styles, rather than a strict adherence to the original. Neoclassicism and Gothic Revival were major parts of this Romanticism. Buildings were also constructed in Baroque Revival and Romanesque Revival, and influenced by Indian, Chinese, Egyptian, and Moorish designs. Romanticism saw the rise of fantastic, whimsical architecture that combined the exotic with native sensibilities.

▲ A riot of red, blue, and yellow, the domed and turreted Palacio da Pena in Portugal was built with a mix of Moorish, Manueline, and medieval motifs

▲ Russian Revival was a melding of Byzantine and early Russian Baroque styles. This gave rise to buildings as varied as (from left to right) the Church of the Dormition, the Great Kremlin Palace, and the Cathedral of Saints Peter and Paul

 ## Gründerzeit

In Germany, Gründerzeit (meaning, founding period) refers to the prosperous times after the Franco-Prussian War of 1870–1871 and the founding of the German Empire in 1871. It was marked by a renewed interest in Germanic heritage. The well-to-do middle class showed off their new-found wealth with richly decorated and furnished houses. This is particularly seen in the works of Max Arwed Rossbach, who was inspired by historic architectural styles.

▶ The unique Palais Rossbach is an architectural jewel of Leipzig, Germany

⊚ Incredible Individuals

In the 1870s, Russian architects looked to their folk culture for inspiration. They glorified peasant architecture and created vivid and intricately decorated palaces and towers of wood. This Russian Revival style was founded by the brilliant Ivan Ropet. Sadly, few of these wonders remain today.

Fairytale Castles

In the early 19th century, the Grimm Brothers published their famous collection of gothic folktales. Inspired by such fairytales, new castle-like buildings cropped up with turrets, pinnacles, small windows and wonky roofs. The most amazing fairytale castle is Neuschwanstein in Germany. Built by King Ludwig II of Bavaria, this dreamy palace is nestled in forested mountains that overlook a sheer gorge. The castle came from an imaginative painting by stage designer and painter, Christian Jank (1833–1888). It was turned into an architecturally sound Romanesque plan by Eduard Riedel (1813–1885). In 1874, Georg von Dollmann became the castle's chief architect; he was replaced by Julius Hofmann in 1886.

Incredible Individuals

Ludwig II of Bavaria, nicknamed "Mad King Ludwig", preferred spending his time on the arts rather than deal with affairs of the state. Apart from his four castles, he is also famous for his patronage of the gifted German composer Richard Wagner. Though Ludwig was much loved by his people, the politicians despised him. He was ultimately declared insane and removed from the throne. Three days later, he was found drowned under mysterious circumstances.

◄ *This detail from the lavish Throne Room at Neuschwanstein shows Byzantine motifs inspired by the Hagia Sophia (in modern-day Istanbul)*

◄ *Neuschwanstein was the inspiration behind the Sleeping Beauty Castle in Disneyland*

The Brighton Pavilion

In the 18th century, the seaside town of Brighton was a popular resort for the rich. Prince George (later, King George IV of Great Britain) hired an architect named Henry Holland (1745–1806) to rebuild his Brighton home into a villa. But the project rapidly grew in scope. The Prince, who was fascinated by the mysterious East, imported lavish furnishings, curios, and hand-painted wallpapers from China. In 1815, he handed over the project to John Nash, who transformed the house into a fantastic oriental palace. Nash turned the exterior into an Indian-inspired conglomeration of minarets and domes. The palace even used cast iron during its construction. Inside, it was an opulent labyrinth of rooms, corridors, and galleries.

▼ *George IV's Royal Pavilion at Brighton*

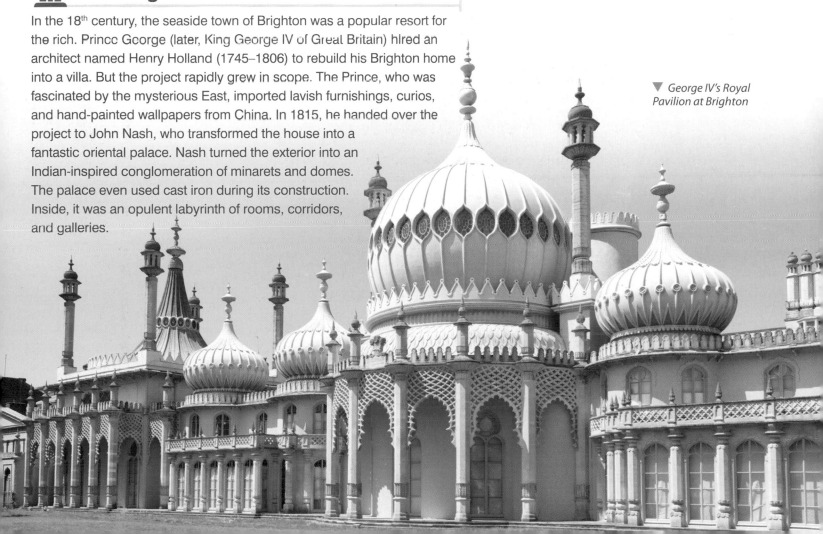

Gothic Revival

Gothic Revival was one of the most influential movements of the 18th century. It came about through the influence of Romantic literature in England. At this time, dramatic novels and poems with Gothic themes were popular. They inspired both the aristocracy and the wealthy middle class. People who had the time and means to indulge their fantasies began to commission Gothic-inspired buildings. Houses with castle-like battlements and turrets began cropping up all over England, especially towards the end of the century. The style soon spread to Europe, North America, and even Australia.

▼ The Basilica of Saint Clotilde is perhaps Paris's first great neo-Gothic structure. It was designed by architect François-Christian Gau (1790–1853) and completed by his partner Théodore Ballu by 1857

▲ St. Paul's Cathedral in Melbourne, Australia was designed by the English Gothic Revival architect William Butterfield towards the end of the 19th century

▲ Church of Saint Peter and Saint Paul at Ostend, Belgium, created in Gothic Revival during 1899–1908

Neo-Gothic Architecture

The 19th century saw the rise of a more serious and studied Gothic style of architecture. This was closer to the original medieval version. It is sometimes called neo-Gothic, to set it apart from the earlier, more frivolous forms of Gothic Revival. Neo-Gothic had a significant impact on the landscape of Europe and North America. With centuries of advances in building technology, more Gothic structures were constructed during the 19th and 20th centuries than during medieval times.

⊙ Incredible Individuals

Gothic Revivalism became a trend after the English writer Horace Walpole (1717–1797) published his medieval thriller, *The Castle of Otranto*. Walpole's own home, Strawberry Hill, was modified over several years by several architects. It is a fanciful Gothic-inspired estate with artificial ruins, asymmetrical buildings, towers, stained-glass windows, and even elements of chinoiserie and Rococo.

▶ A section of Horace Walpole's Gothic Revival home, Strawberry Hill

🏛 The Palace of Westminster

Located on the north bank of the River Thames, the beautiful Palace of Westminster has been the meeting place for the Parliament of the UK since the 13th century. The structure was almost destroyed by a huge fire in 1834. The reconstruction of the palace was turned into an architectural competition. The person with the winning design was Charles Barry (1795–1860). He planned the new buildings in the Gothic Revival style. Most of what remained of the old palace became a part of this new, much larger construction. The palace now holds over 1,100 rooms which are laid out symmetrically around two series of courtyards. The iconic structure of the new palace is the Elizabeth Tower, better known by the nickname of its Great Bell—Big Ben.

 The Great Bell of Big Ben weighs 13,760 kilograms, and is 2.28 metres tall and 2.75 metres wide

🏛 The Gothic Skyscraper

With the 20th century came amazing technologies such as light bulbs and lifts. At the same time, steel replaced stone as the main load-bearing material. Some architects combined steel frameworks with decorative Gothic motifs to create incredible, new age buildings. This can be seen in architect Cass Gilbert's 1913 skyscraper, the Woolworth Building in New York.

◀ *For almost 20 years, the Woolworth Building was the world's tallest skyscraper. Despite its Gothic ornamentation, it represented cutting-edge architecture with the most advanced system of lifts*

🧑 In Real Life

The Palace of Westminster was bombed on 14 different occasions during WWII. Many parts of it, such as the Commons Chamber, had to be reconstructed after the war. The building also underwent massive conservation work to reverse the effects of air pollution.

▲ *Charles Barry's Commons Chamber was destroyed by German bombs during WWII*

New-Age Iron and Glass

In the 19th and early 20th centuries, inventors were making fascinating machines which allowed for mass production of goods. As machines became part of the workforce, new types of buildings were constructed to accommodate them. These included different kinds of factories, power plants, warehouses, department stores, offices, and exhibition halls, to name just a few. New infrastructure, capable of handling machines, also had to be built. Hangars, garages, telephone stations, railway and bus stations; and new types of bridges, tunnels, and roads were needed. Architects and engineers of this booming industrial time invented amazing techniques using iron, steel, glass, and concrete. In 1851, Sir Joseph Paxton's landmark Crystal Palace in London showed how iron and glass could be used to build delicate yet lofty spaces.

▲ Penn Station, New York, around 1936

▲ Henri Labrouste's extraordinary nine-domed iron-and-glass reading room (1860–1867) at the Bibliothèque Nationale, Paris

◀ Constructed by Abraham Darby III over 1777–1779, Iron Bridge is the world's first major cast-iron bridge. It runs across the River Severn in Shropshire, England, and is now closed to vehicles but still used by pedestrians

Crystal Palace, London

Designed by Sir Joseph Paxton, the Crystal Palace was a building made entirely of wrought-iron, with walls made of 300,000 panes of glass. The main body was 563 metres long, 124 metres wide, and 33 metres high at its centre. It had a floor area of about 92,000 m², which drew about 14,000 British and international exhibitors. Among the fascinating things on display were false teeth, steam engines, Colt's repeating pistol, the Koh-i-Noor and Daria-i-Noor diamonds, and many other raw and finished products.

▲ The Crystal Palace in Hyde Park, London

🏛 The Eiffel Tower

Built over 1887–1889, the Eiffel Tower was built in preparation of the Exposition Universelle held in Paris in 1889. The event marked the 100th year of the French Revolution. The company that built the tower was owned by the engineer Gustave Eiffel. The tower was originally designed by Maurice Koechlin and Emile Nouguier, two engineers working in Eiffel's company. Stephen Sauvestre, the company's head architect, added decorative motifs, including the arches at the base and the glass pavilion on the first level. The Eiffel Tower is made of 18,038 metal parts and 7,300 tons of iron. It was built by 150–300 workers on the site, apart from the 50 engineers and designers.

💡 Isn't It Amazing!

At 324 metres, the Eiffel Tower was the tallest structure in the world until 1930, when the Chrysler Building was erected in New York. The tower is not always this high, though. In cold weather, it shrinks by about 6 inches.

▶ As a notable engineer, Gustave Eiffel also contributed to building the Statue of Liberty

▲ The Eiffel Tower was supposed to be a temporary structure and was scheduled to be dismantled in 1909!

🏛 A Chocolate Factory

Menier Chocolate was a chocolate-producing company founded in France in 1816, when chocolate was often used as a medicinal product. During the 1860s, they hired architect Jules Saulnier (1817–1881) to create new buildings for the expanding business. One of these, the Turbine mill, built in 1871 is the first building to have a fully iron skeleton. The infill walls were non-load-bearing. The building was constructed directly over the River Marne and beautifully painted in patterns of yellow-browns and grey-blues. This iconic construction of the Industrial Era is now on the tentative list of UNESCO to be named a World Heritage Site.

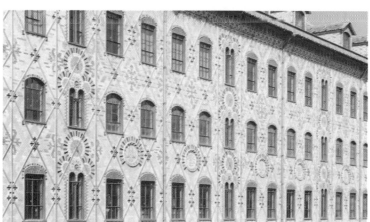

▲ The amazing Saulnier building of the Menier Chocolate Factory

Beaux-Arts

The Ecole des Beaux-Arts (School of Fine Arts) in Paris gave its name to an amazing form of architecture that flourished over the 19th and early 20th centuries. Beaux-Arts architecture was inspired by Neoclassicism, but broke free from its most severe forms. It did so by using Gothic elements and industrial-age materials like glass, wrought-iron, and steel. The style became immensely popular in the Americas. In the USA, it was promoted by numerous American architects who had studied at the Beaux-Arts school. This included the celebrated Henry Hobson Richardson.

▲ Built at the end of the 19th century, the Water Company Palace (Palacio de Aguas Corrientes) is a Beaux-Arts gem of Buenos Aires, Argentina

 ## Grand Palais des Champs-Élysées

This Beaux-Arts work was built by the architects Albert Louvet, Henri Deglane, Albert Thomas, and Charles Girault. The exhibition hall and museum is a vaulting, modern structure of glass, iron, and steel hidden behind an ornate stone facade.

▶ The entrance to the Grand Palais, with its glass and metal domes rising behind

 ## Origins of Beaux-Arts

The formality of Neoclassicism fell out of favour with some teachers at the French academy. This included men like Joseph-Louis Duc (1802–1879), Henri Labrouste (1801–1875) and Leon Vaudoyer (1803–1872). Around this time, there was a renewed interest in the Middle Ages. By including elements from the Middle Ages, the architects wanted to create a more original French style of architecture. Breaking away from Rome, they wished to produce architecture imbued with their own national character.

▲ Setting the trend for modern library architecture, Henri Labrouste's Bibliothèque Nationale de France

▲ Sainte-Geneviève Library in Paris looks austerely. Classical on the outside, it is full of innovative and glorious metalwork and glass-work inside

▲ One of the two amazing Fontaines de la Concorde in the Place de la Concorde, Paris. Designed by Jacques Hittorff, it was finished in 1840 (during the reign of King Louis-Philippe)

Beaux-Arts in the USA

In America, Beaux-Arts is more closely associated with Greco Roman revivalism. Over 1880–1930, it led to some of the most lofty, extravagant, and awe-inspiring buildings in the country. Beaux Arts set trends for modern America by constructing public structures that are still in use today. This includes museums, universities, and even railway stations. Early architects of the style include the gifted Richard Morris Hunt and Henry Hobson Richardson. They brought the style back to the USA and inspired a generation of eager architectural students.

▶ The majestic Grand Central Terminal In New York was designed in the Beaux-Arts style to serve as a gateway to the city. Designed by the firms Reed & Stem and Warren & Wetmore, numerous artists and architects worked on the building until its completion in 1913

▲ Designed by Richard Morris Hunt and completed at the turn of the 20th century, the Great Hall is part of the Beaux-Arts building of the Metropolitan Museum of Art, the largest art museum in the USA

Richardsonian Romanesque

Henry Hobson Richardson (1838–1886) became famous for a distinct type of architecture named Richardsonian Romanesque, seen in his amazing Trinity Church in Boston.

▶ Trinity Church shows the developing aesthetics of the USA. It stands on the same square as the Boston Public Library, a Beaux-Arts landmark

Art Nouveau

Art Nouveau is the name given to a decorative style that flourished for a brief period between 1890 and 1910. It was marked by the late 19th century love for all things new and original. Architects of the time produced rich and flowing designs, deliberately free from historical influence.

They created sinuous, asymmetrical, and swirling works using iron, glass, and other materials. Art Nouveau also affected interior design and commercial art (like poster and jewellery designs).

▲ A bed and mirror by Gustave Serrurier-Bovy (1858–1910), the Belgian architect and furniture designer who pioneered the Art Nouveau style

▲ Maison Hankar, home of the early Art Nouveau architect Paul Hankar (1859–1901)

▲ This dragonfly corsage of gold, enamel and diamonds was made by René Lalique, one of Paris's leading Art Nouveau jewellery designers

🏛 An International Theme

Art Nouveau is a French term. It began in England where it was inspired by Romantic literature and Pre-Raphaelite painters. The movement spread to other parts of Europe, developing regional variations. In Germany, the style was called *Jugendstil*; in Austria it was called *Sezessionstil*; in Italy it was called *Stile Floreale;* and in Spain, *Modernismo*.

▲ The Peacock Room by James Whistler shows the burgeoning aesthetics of Art Nouveau

Art Nouveau in France

The 1900 Paris Exposition held in the
Beaux-Arts Grand Palais (*see pp 22*)
exhibited a treasure-trove of Art Nouveau
furniture, glassware, jewellery, and other
decorative crafts. It made Paris the
international centre for the Art Nouveau
style. Soon, extraordinary new structures of
iron, masonry, and concrete began to rise
on the French landscape. This included
the Paris Metro entrance gates designed
by the influential young architect, Hector
Guimard (1867–1942). Pioneering architect
Anatole de Baudot (1834–1915) built the
Church of Saint-Jean de Montmartre using
reinforced concrete and steel rods; it was
the first church to be constructed in this
manner. Russian-born Parisian Xavier
Schoellkopf (1869–1911) built a fabulous
Art Nouveau house for the singer and actress,
Yvette Guilbert. Even a Paris department store,
La Samaritaine, was built in the new style,
designed by Frantz Jourdain (1847–1935).

▲ *Wrought-iron Art Nouveau entrance of the
Paris metro station*

▲ *Art Nouveau doorway by architect Jules
Lavirotte (1864–1924) with sculptures by
Jean-François Larrivé (1875–1928)*

Victor Horta (1861–1947)

The Belgian architect and designer Victor Horta is often
considered the champion of the Art Nouveau movement. His
earliest work in the style is the four-storied Hôtel Tassel (1892–
1893) in Brussels. Its octagonal hall and curved staircase are
characteristic of Art Nouveau. The architect's preference for such
curvilinear and tendril-like forms is also seen in the sophisticated
Hôtel Solvay, Hôtel van Eetvelde, and Horta's own home. His best-
known work was the Maison du Peuple. It was the first building in
Belgium to be designed with so much iron and glass on its facade.
Sadly, this Art Nouveau gem was demolished in the 1965 to make
way for a skyscraper.

▶ *The stairway at Hôtel Tassel*

 *Jugendstil* and *Sezessionstil*

The flexible, S-shaped ornamental style, called whiplash or eel
style, was common in *Jugendstil* and *Sezessionstil* designs. This
can be seen in Munich's Hofatelier Elvira, created by August
Endell (1871–1925) and Vienna's Majolikahaus, created by
Otto Wagner (1841–1918). Wagner's student Josef Hoffmann
designed Stoclet House in Brussels. This asymmetrical white
masterpiece is now a UNESCO World Heritage Site. Eliel
Saarinen brought Art Nouveau to Finland with his designs
for the Helsinki Central Railway Station.

▶ *Whiplash motifs on the facade of Majolikahaus*

Defying Tradition

In the early 20th century, many architects came up with bold new designs that were inspired by traditional architecture, yet seemed to defy tradition. Some of these came from using modern materials like steel and concrete to build old designs like medieval towers and Classical arches. In many cases, the originality came by mixing different architectural traditions to create buildings of amazing originality.

▲ The Rashtrapati Bhavan (Presidential Palace) at New Delhi was designed in a mix of Indo-Saracenic and English Baroque architectural style by Edwin Lutyens (1869–1944)

▲ Designed by Jewish-German architect Erich Mendelsohn (1887–1953), the futuristic Einstein Tower in Potsdam was built over 1919–1921 to house a solar telescope. Einstein never worked here but is said to have approved of the brick and stucco structure as being organic

 ## Karl Marx Hof

At the end of WWI, Vienna began building hordes of apartments for its impoverished working classes. The largest of these was the Karl Marx Hof, built over 1927–1930. Designed by the architect Karl Ehn, it stretched for 1.1 km and remains the longest single residential building in the world. The building held 1,382 apartments, plus laundromats, public baths, playschools, a library, a surgical clinic, and office spaces. Around it were playgrounds and gardens. The fortress-like building with its spikes and turrets became an actual holdout, when, in 1934, it became a battleground in the Austrian Civil War.

⊙ Incredible Individuals

In 1931, Germany was chosen to host the Olympic Games in 1936. Under orders from Hitler, architect Werner March and his brother Walter designed the gigantic Olympiastadion using a modern steel framework disguised in 'classical' stone. Hitler and his comrades watched the 1936 games from a special stand. His flawed beliefs in Aryan supremacy and Übermensch (Superhumans) were proven wrong before the whole world, when African American athlete Jesse Owens won four gold medals.

▲ Olympiastadion, Berlin, 1936

▲ Karl Marx Hof, designed in a rationalistic and functional style, is so long that it spans four tram stops

Chilehaus

Built in what is called **Brick Expressionism**, Chilehaus is a massive 1920s office complex with 10 storeys. Designed by architect Fritz Höger (1877–1949) for a shipping magnate, the formidable building curves fluidly in the shape of a ship. The sharp angle at the tip—the nose of the 'ship'—is the most acute architectural bend in Europe. Occupying an incredible 5,950 m², Chilehaus is made of **reinforced concrete** and 4.8 million bricks. Because it is located on unstable land close to a river, the foundation had to be made secure. This was done by building concrete pilings that were 16 metres deep. Chilehaus has one of the few functioning **paternoster** lifts in the world.

▲ The ship-shape, brick marvel of the 1920s, Chilehaus

Moscow Metro

Built on Stalin's orders, the Moscow metro stations are lavish constructions of marble, chandeliers, mosaics, and sculptures. Constructed underneath the city streets from the 1930s onwards, these ambitious projects showcase Russian architectural talent. The designs were guided by the principles of *svet* (light) and *sveltloe budushchee* (bright future). The station Ploshchad Revolyutsii, created by Alexey Dushkin, features 76 bronze sculptures. They depict Russian soldiers, farmers, workers, children, and famous individuals. The glittering Mayakovskaya station is famous for its 34 ceiling mosaics that show '24 Hours in the Land of the Soviets'. The white and gold Kievskaya station is dedicated to the friendship between Russia and Ukraine. It is named after Ukraine's capital, Kiev.

▲ The spectacular and futuristic Elektrozavodskaya station

▲ Social themes displayed in the art at Kievskaya station

Antoni Gaudí

The Spanish architect Antoni Gaudí i Cornet (1852–1926) had a unique style that defies categorisation. Gaudí loved the outdoors. Inspired by nature, he avoided designing buildings with straight lines. He analysed natural phenomena and living forms. Through this, he developed ways to build structures that curved and flowered in complex shapes. Such organic architecture had never been seen in the world before. Gaudí also decorated his creations with intense and symbolic details made from ceramics, tiles, stained glass, wrought-iron, and woodwork.

▲ The miraculous vaulted nave at the Sagrada Família, Gaudí's crowning achievement, symbolises trees rising up to the roof

▲ One of the painted, gated entrances at the fantastic Casa Milà, a UNESCO World Heritage Site

 Park Güell

Situated on top of a hill overlooking a sea, Park Güell was built over 1900–1914 as a private estate, and later opened to the public in 1926. This is one of Gaudí's early works in a naturalistic style. To build the park on the slopes, Gaudí analysed and invented amazing new geometrical solutions. This allowed him to make buildings in free-flowing designs that seemed one with nature. Gaudí's vivid imagination gave rise to many unique spaces, including undulating roads, a strangely tilted gallery, fairytale-like buildings by the entrance, an open hall with a forest of columns, and a number of statues, mosaics and fountains. Possibly the most popular spot is the main terrace, which is surrounded by a long bench shaped like a sea serpent.

▲ Park Guell's giant salamander mosaic nicknamed El Drac (The Dragon) is one of Gaudí's most well-known works

▲ Seen from the serpentine terrace, the whimsical buildings by the Park Guell entrance resembles gingerbread houses with meringue roofs and candied towers

▲ Unique, titled pillars support a road that follows the slope of a hill

Casa Batlló

Gaudí's Casa Batlló began as a renovation of an older, more conventional house that had four storeys. In the end, it transformed into a poetic, otherworldly construction. Gaudí changed the exterior by adding large oval windows on the first floor. Their frames are interrupted by long slender pillars in the shape of bones. Balconies on the floors above match this skeletal theme by resembling half-skulls with tilted openings for eyes. The entire bone-coloured facade is decorated with bright, multicoloured mosaics that resemble a lake of water lilies. Inside, Gaudí arranged the spaces and stairways to allow greater light and ventilation. The whole building is crowned with an amazing roof shaped like the back of a dragon resting against a stack of chimneys.

▲ The one-of-a-kind Casa Batlló

Incredible Individuals

A Roman Catholic, Gaudí held deep beliefs that he expressed in religious and symbolic imagery. He was also a kind human being who built schools and hospitals for his workers and their children. Under Pope John Paul II, Gaudí was officially named a 'Servant of God' in 2003.

◄ In 1902, Romantic artist Joan Llimona painted Saint Philip Neri using Gaudí as the model for the saint

▼ The spectacular Basilica of la Sagrada Família

Sagrada Família

The curvilinear Basilica of la Sagrada Família was Gaudí's last and greatest work. It was unfinished at the time of his death and is still under construction. Gaudí's design had 18 towers—12 representing the apostles, 4 for the evangelists, 1 for the Virgin Mary and 1 for Jesus Christ. The ornate Nativity facade, which faces the northeast, depicts the birth of Christ. It is surmounted by four towers of the apostles. The more austere Passion facade faces the setting sun and shows the suffering of Christ during the crucifixion. It bears the four other towers that have been constructed. Lifts inside the building take the visitors to the highest points.

Skyscrapers

The term 'skyscrapers' was first used during the 1880s. It was meant to describe buildings that were at least 10 storeys high. These first appeared in the USA. Early forms of the skyscraper were built with sturdy masonry at the ground level. This was later replaced by iron frameworks that could take the weight of higher floors. In the 1860s, a new way of processing steel—which is lighter and stronger than iron—led to the first true skyscrapers.

◀ The stylish Chrysler Building was the world's tallest building for a mere 11 months before the Empire State Building stole its limelight. The latter's architect sneakily bolted a spire on top of the Empire State Building to make it taller than the Chrysler. Here's an iconic image of a worker on the Empire State Building with the Chrysler Building behind him

▲ New York's Metropolitan Life Insurance Building (1909) was designed by Napoleon Le Brun after St Mark's Campanile, a famous bell tower in Venice

Elevators

A number of technological and social changes brought the skyscraper into existence. Key among them was the invention of the safety elevator, by Elisha Otis, in the mid 19th century. The safety feature allowed the lift to carry passengers safely, without the fear of cables breaking. The first safety elevator was installed in the E.V. Haughwout & Co. store, New York, in 1857. It was powered by steam, not electricity. And it was effective for buildings that were only about 4–5 storeys high.

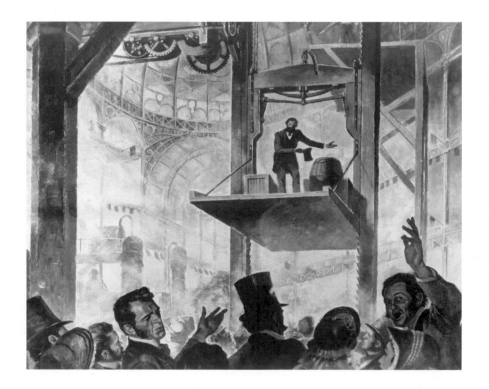

Isn't It Amazing!

While skyscrapers were multiplying rapidly in 19th century Chicago and New York, things were a little different in London. Queen Victoria had complained that tall buildings obstructed the view. Thus, architects were forced to stick to lower heights. This rule continues to exist today, with a few exceptions.

▲ London's first skyscraper, 55 Broadway, was built by architect Charles Holden. Constructed over 1927–1929, it was the new HQ for the electric railways and still houses the Transport for London offices

◀ Elisha Otis demonstrated the safety elevator at the 1853 World's Fair held in New York's Crystal Palace

Early Skyscrapers

One of the earliest buildings to use a metal framework was Oriel Chambers (1864) in Liverpool, England. Designed by Peter Ellis, it was five floors high and featured a glass **curtain wall**. The first skyscraper to use a steel frame was William Le Baron Jenney's 10-storey-high Home Insurance Building (1884–1885) in Chicago. It was soon followed by Burnham and Root's 45-metre-high, all-steel Rand McNally Building (1889) in the same city. In St. Louis, Missouri, the 10-storey-high Wainwright Building (1891) was designed by Dankmar Adler and Louis Sullivan. Its honeycomb of office windows were separated by vertical shafts inspired by Classical architecture. This design emphasized the soaring nature of the skyscraper. It is considered the father of modern-day office buildings.

▲ *Oriel Chambers with its glass curtain wall*

Flatiron Building

The triangular, 22-storey Flatiron Building in New York is one of the most dramatic landmarks of the city. It was designed by Chicago architect and urban planner Daniel Burnham (1846–1912) and designer Frederick P. Dinkelberg. Construction was completed in 1902. With a terracotta and limestone facade, the building has a Beaux-Arts style with French and Renaissance influences. The narrow end of the triangle is less than 2 metre wide.

In Real Life

The 102-storey Empire State Building was designed by the architectural firm Shreve, Lamb & Harmon. When it was completed in 1931, the building was 381 metre high. When its antenna was added in 1950, the total height came up to 449 metre, but reduced to 443 metre when the antenna was replaced. It was the tallest building in the world for 40 years until the World Trade Centre was built.

▲ *The Empire State Building as seen from across the East River*

▲ *The Flatiron Building towering over Manhattan*

MODERN ART

PRE-MODERN AND MODERN ART

As we get closer to modern times, art history becomes more complex. The advancements of the modern period made it easier to travel and exchange materials and ideas. Thus, we find artists exploring different styles of art over their lifetime. They are no longer limited to a single period. Pablo Picasso, for instance, is considered to be one of the founders of Cubism. Yet, he also painted Neoclassical and Surreal pieces. Many of the artists mentioned in this book similarly experimented with different styles and mediums. Be sure to investigate the ones that catch your eye as you will be amazed by what you may discover!

▼ *The Old Guitarist (1903) and L'Aubade (1942) show two very different styles of modern art, executed by Picasso*

Baroque Art

Originating in Rome, baroque art bloomed over c.1590–1720. It rose in reaction to the strict rules of Renaissance art. It was also powered by the Catholic Church, which was trying to regain its influence over the western world. Baroque art is theatrical and stylistically complex. The works are dramatic, dynamic, and emotionally intense.

▲ *St Joseph the Carpenter (c. 1642) is a glowing piece of art by French baroque painter Georges de La Tour. Full of Christian symbolism, it shows a young Jesus with his earthly father, Joseph*

🏛 Bernini's David

Baroque master Gian Lorenzo Bernini (1598–1680) captured a moment of biblical drama with *David*. As he prepares to catapult the fatal stone at his enemy Goliath, David is coiled with aggressive tension, his body twisted like a spring and his face furrowed in concentration. Only 24 years old at that time, Bernini broke the mould with this creation. Unlike previous self-contained sculptures of David—by Donatello and Michelangelo—Bernini's dynamic piece interacts with the space around it.

◀ *The life-size marble masterpiece David (1623–1624), by baroque architect and sculptor Gian Lorenzo Bernini*

🏛 Alessandro Algardi

High baroque sculptor Alessandro Algardi (1598–1654) rivalled Bernini with his creations. One of his best-known works is the gigantic relief-sculpture at St Peter's Basilica in Rome called the *Meeting of Attila and Pope Leo.*

◀ *Algardi's dramatic Fuga d'Attila (1646–53) gave an immeasurable boost to the art of creating marble reliefs*

🏛 Caravaggism

Although not a baroque painter himself, the Italian artist Caravaggio (1571–1610) had a huge impact on the movement. His techniques of **tenebrism** and **chiaroscuro** were widely copied by such baroque masters as Rembrandt and Diego Velázquez.

Artemisia Gentileschi (1593–c. 1653)

Influenced by Caravaggism, Artemisia Gentileschi became one of the most famous female baroque masters. She was the first female artist elected into the Academy of the Arts of Drawing in Florence. Her amazing biblical art can be seen in *Judith Beheading Holofernes* (1620). It was considered a high point in baroque art.

◀ *The macabre biblical scene of Judith Beheading Holofernes (1614–1620) by Artemisia Gentileschi*

⭐ Incredible Individuals

Among Gentileschi's notable female predecessors were the Renaissance artist Sofonisba Anguissola (1532–1625) and Mannerist master Barbara Longhi (1552–1638). The portrait painter Lavinia Fontana (1552–1614) was the first woman to paint female nudes.

▶ *Fontana's Minerva Dressing (1613) shows the Roman Goddess of wisdom and war*

🏛 The Surrender of Breda

Diego Velázquez (1599–1660), court painter to King Philip IV, dominated Spanish baroque art. His *The Surrender of Breda* marks the military victory of his friend, the famed Spanish General Don Ambrogio Spinola, over the city of Breda (in Holland). Magnanimous Spinola set honourable terms for the defeated party. The painting shows him dismounting from his horse and meeting the Dutch leader as an equal. This showed that Spain wished for friendship with the Dutch party. Commissioned by the king in 1635, the painting was one of the 12 battle scenes meant to decorate the throne room of the Buen Retiro Palace.

▲ *The Surrender of Breda, c. 1635*

Francisco de Zurbarán 🏛 (1598–1664)

The devout Zurbarán painted serious, intense images influenced by Quietism, which is a Catholic movement rooted in submissive silence and penitential tasks. Zurbarán's mystical paintings of Saint Francis of Assisi are his best-known works. His creations use the shadowy textures of Caravaggism but are tinged with positive light. This gives the paintings a reserved yet emphatic feel.

▶ *St. Francis in Meditation (1632), a painting by Zurbarán*

Rubens (1577–1640)

The Flemish master Peter Paul Rubens is considered to be the most important baroque artist of northern Europe. A devout Catholic, Rubens believed that kings ruled by divine right. In addition to these deep convictions, his undeniable talent, classical scholarship, and consistent diplomacy made him a favourite with the powers of Europe. He was eagerly sought after by the Church and State alike to portray their causes. The bulk of Rubens's work is thus, religious, historical, and mythological. His paintings are amazing pieces of movement and colour.

▲ *The Fall of Phaeton, c. 1604, shows Zeus punishing Phaeton with thunderbolts for stealing the chariot of the Sun God, while the Hours and Seasons cower in terror. The horses were inspired by the drawings of Renaissance artist Leonardo da Vinci*

▲ *The Fall of the Damned, c. 1620, depicts a scene from the Last Judgement according to the Gospel of Matthew: 'Depart from me, ye cursed, into the eternal fire that is prepared for the devil and his angels'*

Samson and Delilah

A deceptively peaceful work, Rubens's *Samson and Delilah* shows yet another biblical tale. It depicts the Jewish hero Samson in deep sleep. The woman he loves, Delilah, has brought in servants to cut off his hair. Samson's hair is the source of his extraordinary strength. Without his hair, he would be easily captured by his enemies—the Philistine soldiers lurking behind the door. Rubens's painting is full of symbols. A statue of Venus and Cupid, the gods of love, stands in a corner. They indicate that love will be the cause of Samson's destruction. The barber's hands are crossed, representing deceit. Despite the large resting man in the centre, the scene is full of tension created by the masterful play of shadows and light.

▲ *Rubens's Samson and Delilah (1609–1610) is an oil sketch on a wood panel. Another version of it exists as an ink-and-wash drawing on paper. The old woman behind Delilah is not part of the Bible story. She is thought to symbolise Delilah's grim future*

 Incredible Individuals

Experts believe that Samson's amazing physique here was inspired by Michelangelo's work, specifically the fresco of God creating Adam, painted on the ceiling of the Sistine Chapel.

The Marie de' Medici Cycle

In 1621, Rubens undertook a series of 24 paintings on the life and glory of Queen Marie de' Medici, the widow of Henry IV of France and the country's effective ruler. The series was an immense undertaking and Rubens did full justice to the paintings. He produced rich, vibrant, and imaginative paintings that showed royalty being celebrated by courtiers and divine beings.

Mythological creatures such as cherubs and nymphs, zodiacal figures like Sagittarius and gods like the all-powerful Saturn and the wise Minerva lend epic poetry to the life of the Queen. In the first painting, the Fates foretell her birth; in another, the Graces guide her education. In *The Meeting of Marie de' Medici and Henry IV at Lyons*, the couple is shown as Jupiter and Juno, the king and queen of the Roman gods. The series could have easily been frivolous and even satirical. Yet, Rubens's robust and impeccable style, combined with his genuine belief in the divine, gives these series of paintings a real ceremony and lasting artistic grandeur.

▲ *Marie de' Medici disembarks at Marseilles, France. Fame trumpets her arrival while sea gods and nymphs rise in welcome*

▲ *The Meeting of Marie de' Medici and Henry IV at Lyon; the lions pulling the chariot are a pun on the city's name*

▲ *The Triumph of Juliers shows the only military engagement in which Marie de' Medici took an active part*

▲ *The Coronation in Saint-Denis shows Marie de' Medici being crowned. Her young son and heir, the future Louis XIII of France, stands between her and the cardinal with his back to the viewer. The winged figures of Abundance and Victory shower her with blessings and gold*

The Dutch Golden Age

Baroque-period Holland developed its own art traditions called Dutch Realism. Lasting over 1600–1680, it created the Golden Age of Dutch art. The Protestant artists here preferred everyday subjects to monumental religious themes. They painted landscapes, still life, and portraits using oil paints and **easels**. New schools of art sprang up in towns like Haarlem, Delft, and Amsterdam. The Dutch Golden Age was enormously successful and deeply influenced later Impressionist painters such as Manet and Vincent van Gogh.

▲ *Cook at a Kitchen Table with Dead Game, c. 1634–1637, by Flemish artist Frans Snyders, who powerfully depicted still life and animal subjects in the Dutch Realist style*

▲ *The Bull by Dutchman Paulus Potter used a large canvas for a subject that was neither epic nor historical. Instead, it was sublimely rustic*

🏛 Jacob van Ruisdael (1628–1682)

One of the most gifted baroque masters, Ruisdael completed his first mature painting before he turned 20. Over 1650–1670, he painted innumerable landscapes, from views of Haarlem and changing seasons to woodlands, fields, countrysides, and dramatic seascapes. Ruisdael expressed the cyclical changes in the world. His canvasses reflect the mystical wonder of growth, decay, and the renewal of life. This is best seen in the *Jewish Cemetery*, where a dark scene of tombs, ruins, and gnarled old trunks contrasts with a rainbow and new greenery. Dense clouds, both grey and light, roll over the solemn scene, suggesting movement and change.

◀ *The Jewish Cemetery, c. 1654–1655*

👤 In Real Life

Ruisdael's genius was rarely acknowledged in his lifetime. In 1681, the council of Haarlem was petitioned to allow him into the almshouse for the poor. He died there the following year. As fate would have it, his works fetch millions of dollars today!

🏛 Jan Steen (1629–1679)

No baroque painter has portrayed the relations between children and grown-ups with such charm as Jan Steen. The artist's compositions show great humour and insight. He was sometimes so focused on the subject and expression that he became more of a cartoonist than a painter. Steen's works offer a moral and satirical look into the life of ordinary of his time.

▶ *The World Turned Upside Down (c. 1663), is a typical Jan Steen picture showing the household at play while the housewife sleeps*

🏛 Frans Hals (1582–1666)

The Flemish-born painter Frans Hals was a master portraitist, considered second only to Rembrandt. *The Laughing Cavalier* is his best-known work. Unlike most traditional portraits, which were stiff or serious, this one is imbued with the true presence of the subject. There is an informal lightness to the portrait that sets Hals apart from his fellow artists. *The Meagre Company* is one of his famous military group portraits. However, the painting was completed by the Amsterdam painter Pieter Codde. It is believed that Hals worked on the figures to the right, while Codde finished the group to the left.

▲ *The Meagre Company, completed in 1637, shows militiamen carrying banners and lances*

▲ *Frans Hals's, The Laughing Cavalier (1624) is an iconic baroque portrait*

🏛 Girl with a Pearl Earring

Painted by the brilliant Johannes Vermeer (1632–1675), the *Mona Lisa* of the North is a *tronie*, meaning 'face' in 17th century Dutch. These paintings depicted people with exaggerated expressions or flamboyant costumes. Set in a dark background, the brightly lit girl gazes directly and softly at the viewer. Her expression and the mystery behind her identity has led people to compare this painting to the *Mona Lisa*. Vermeer has used his expertise in representing light to create her form rather than using lines. Vermeer made generous use of ultramarine blue, an expensive colour extracted from the semi-precious stone *lapis lazuli*.

▶ *Girl with a Pearl Earring, c. 1665*

Rembrandt (1606–1669)

The amazing Rembrandt Harmenszoon van Rijn was a supreme portrait artist and a master of Dutch Realism. He worked on a number of subjects and experimented with many styles. The resulting canvasses were wondrous and deeply influenced far-off artists of the period, even though Rembrandt himself never travelled abroad. Rembrandt's prints, allegories, biblical art, and mythological paintings are particularly fine. He also gives us a clear idea of life as it was in 17th century Amsterdam.

▲ The Blinding of Samson is a 1636 painting showing a key moment from the Bible when Samson is blinded by the Philistines

▲ One of the greatest paintings from Rembrandt's later years is the sorrowful Suicide of Lucretia, illustrating the event that led to the overthrow of the Roman monarchy and the establishment of the Republic of Rome

 ## Painting Methods

Like many artists of his time, Rembrandt was influenced by Caravaggio's style. His own paintings were done with thick, broad brushstrokes and used layers of colours for intensity. His mastery over *chiaroscuro* is visible in the portraits and self-portraits. His paintings show both restraint and devotion, typical of Dutch Protestants.

▶ Self-Portrait with Beret and Turned-Up Collar, 1659

 ## The Anatomy Lesson of Doctor Nicolaes Tulp (1632)

A landmark piece in guild portraits, *The Anatomy Lesson of Doctor Nicolaes Tulp* is a striking picture that was commissioned by the Amsterdam Guild of Surgeons. It shows the learned anatomist Dr Tulp dissecting the forearm of a cadaver. He is lecturing the other doctors on how muscles work. Rembrandt broke tradition while drafting this scene. Instead of painting the members grouped around the corpse and looking straight back at the viewer, he chose to portray an actual lesson. Thus, Dr Tulp is clearly speaking to his colleagues. The members look to him and at the corpse with clear interest. The lively composition established the reputation of the 26-year-old Rembrandt as a unique portraitist.

▶ The Anatomy Lesson of Doctor Nicolaes Tulp, 1632

The Night Watch (1642)

Another piece that broke the mould was Rembrandt's painting called *The Night Watch*. Militia companies were usually drawn in neat rows, sitting, or standing. Rembrandt painted this militia with all of its equipment in hand, as if the members were waiting for orders to act. The artist uses *tenebrism* and fluid poses to suggest lively activity. The painting caused a lot of debate by turning an ordinary subject into a dynamic artwork. For a long time, a layer of varnish covered this piece, leading many to think—incorrectly—that the painting was a night scene.

▲ *The Night Watch (1642), painted by Rembrandt at the height of his career*

In Real Life

The amazing *The Storm on the Sea of Galilee* illustrates a biblical tale of Christ teaching his disciples the value of faith in the midst of a deadly storm. In 1990, this priceless treasure was stolen by two thieves who broke into the museum dressed as policemen. To this day, the museum has kept its original frame empty, waiting for the return of the painting.

▲ *The Storm on the Sea of Galilee (1633)*

Incredible Individuals

Within weeks of completing *The Night Watch*, Rembrandt lost his wife and muse, the heiress Saskia van Uylenborch. He was left with an infant son and a large house cluttered with his extravagant purchases. By 1656, he was bankrupt.

Many religious pictures mark this troubled period. *The Supper at Emmaus* expresses the translucent gloom that both veils and reveals Rembrandt's figures in a deeply spiritual manner.

▶ *The Supper at Emmaus (1648) depicts the story of Jesus after his crucifixion. The scene shows a resurrected Christ breaking bread with two disciples who have only just realised who he is*

▲ *Portrait of Saskia van Uylenburgh, c. 1634–1640*

▲ *Rembrandt painted his son Titus as a monk in 1660*

Rococo Art

Under the patronage of King Louis XV (1710–1774) and his mistress Madame de Pompadour, a new art movement developed in France. This light-hearted, even frivolous style became popular in all forms of decorative art—from painting and sculpture to furniture and porcelain. Whimsical, mischievous, and elaborately decorative, it is called the Rococo style.

▲ The work of French furniture maker Charles Cressent (1685–1768), this Rococo chest of drawers was created using rich woods, decorative gilt-bronze mounts, and a marble top

Rococo Artists

Notable figures in Rococo art include Jean-Antoine Watteau (1684–1721), who was famous for his outdoor courtship scenes; Jean-Honoré Fragonard (1732–1806), who painted pictures of love; and Francois Boucher (1703–1770), who was known for his opulent, self-indulgent paintings.

From Venice, Giovanni Battista Tiepolo (1696–1770) earned his fame painting the fabulous frescoes at Würzburg Residence over 1750–1753. The nymph and satyr sculptures of Claude Michel Clodion (1738–1814) belong to this period. Clodion is also remembered as a sculptor of the relief on the Arc de Triomphe du Carrousel. In Britain, Thomas Gainsborough (1727–1788) achieved Rococo excellence in female portraits.

▶ *The Swing (1767), by Jean-Honoré Fragonard, is a typically mischievous Rococo painting of a young man peeking up at a woman while she swings high and sends her skirts and shoe flying into the air*

The Pilgrimage to Cythera

An **allegory** of falling in love, the *Pilgrimage to Cythera* belonged to a new genre of painting called the *fête galante*, which displayed playful outdoor gatherings. The painting expresses the elegant courtliness fashionable in Louis XV's France. In Classical mythology, Cythera is the birthplace of Venus, the goddess of love. Watteau's painting shows young people who have sailed to Cythera to find love. Some believe that the lovers have already met and are about to leave Cythera and return home. The entire painting has a wavy, rhythmic structure that conveys liveliness. The dreamy atmosphere, the peeping statue of Venus, the flying cherubs, all combine in beautiful contrasting shades to make this a Rococo masterpiece.

▲ *Pilgrimage to Cythera, c. 1717 by Jean-Antoine Watteau*

Elisabeth Vigée Le Brun (1755–1842)

Completely self-taught, the gifted Elisabeth Vigée Le Brun became the court portraitist to Queen Marie-Antoinette of France. At a time when it was hard for women to become professional artists, Le Brun was a huge success. Her best works are portraits of women, including herself. She painted with a gentle, flattering style, which made her popular with Europe's nobility. Le Brun painted towards the end of the Rococo period and soon abandoned the style to become one of the earliest Neoclassical artists.

⊛ Incredible Individuals

François Boucher painted mythological scenes, particularly nudes, with great wit and charm. The influential French philosopher Denis Diderot (1713–1784) said of him, 'That man is capable of everything—except the truth.'

▶ Boucher's 1756 portrait of Madame de Pompadour

▲ Elisabeth Vigée Le Brun's Self-portrait in a Straw Hat, 1782, has the lively, light colours of Rococo, and the composition and proportions of early Neoclassicism

🏛 The Blue Boy (c. 1770)

One of Britain's most influential landscape artists, Thomas Gainsborough was also a talented portrait painter. *The Blue Boy* shows a combination of both these styles. In the background, Gainsborough painted a moody sky and the dark, tree-covered slope of a mountain. The boy is drawn standing confidently in **contrapposto**. His shiny clothes are drawn in great detail. The painting is in fact a costume study. It shows the frilly attire and shoes popular among boys and girls of this time. In contrast are the feathered male hat and bold pose, which show that the boy is on the verge of becoming a man.

🏛 Reynold's Grand Style

Gainsborough's greatest rival was the talented portrait painter Sir Joshua Reynolds. Influenced by Dutch, Flemish, and Renaissance masters, Reynolds tried to further the grand style of painting using rich, harmonious compositions without unnecessary detail and distractions.

▶ The Countess of Harrington's 1778–1779 portrait displays an air of icy self-confidence and expresses the grand style of Joshua Reynolds

▲ The Blue Boy, c. 1770, is believed to be a portrait of Jonathan Buttall, the son of a wealthy hardware merchant

Neoclassical Art

Neoclassicism was the popular art form of Europe throughout the late 18th and early 19th centuries. This was the Age of Enlightenment when Europe looked for reason and order. It was naturally inspired by the kindred spirit of Ancient Greece and Ancient Rome. Neoclassicism also arose in reaction to the grandiose baroque and frivolous Rococo art forms. In contrast, Neoclassical paintings and sculptures were serious. They portrayed heroic and self-sacrificial figures from Greek and Roman legend, often in stern forms and sombre colours. The art was meant to convey the generation's high moral values.

▲ *Le Triomphe de 1810 is a high relief sculpture created by the French artist Jean-Pierre Cortot (1787–1843) on the Arc de Triomphe in Paris*

▲ *A Neoclassical masterpiece, Oath of the Horatii (1784) by the celebrated painter Jacques-Louis David (1748–1825) shows a scene from a Roman tale, and expresses patriotism and self-sacrifice for one's nation*

 ## Anton Raphael Mengs (1728–1779)

Known as the German Raphael, the Rococo artist Mengs was a founding master of Neoclassical painting. He was a court painter in Saxony and Madrid. His contemporaries held him to be the greatest painter alive. Mengs worked largely on portraits. He also produced altarpieces, prayer items, and large frescos as seen in the Royal Palace of Madrid. Perhaps his most famous work is the fresco called *Parnassus* on the ballroom ceiling at Villa Albani, Rome.

◀ *Mengs's Parnassus (1761), is a painting of the mythical Mount Parnassus, home of the Greek god Apollo, shown here surrounded by the Muses*

🏛 Angelica Kauffman (1741–1807)

Another founder of Neoclassicism, Angelica Kauffman was acclaimed by scholars of her time. She became famous with her Rococo portraits but soon moved on to more Classical pieces. Her famous 1790 painting shows the goddess Venus convincing Queen Helen of Sparta to run away with Prince Paris of Troy. This event sparked the Trojan War narrated in Homer's Greek epic poem, *The Iliad*.

▲ *Venus inducing Helen to fall in love with Paris, made in 1790 by Angelica Kauffman*

👤✓ In Real Life

In 1768, Angelica Kauffman and fellow artist Mary Moser became two of the founding members of the Royal Academy of Arts in London. Even though they set the academy with the men, women were excluded from it for the next hundred years. As a result, it lost great talents like the wartime painter Elizabeth Thompson (1846–1933).

In 1860, the academy accepted an application from the worthy L. Herford, not realising that she was a woman! Even as late as 1980, there were only eight women in the academy. In 2020, the Serbian artist Marina Abramovic will become the first woman to have a solo show across the main galleries of the academy.

▲ *An 1802 print of the Royal Academicians Assembled in their Council Chamber, to Adjudge the Medals to the Successful Students in Painting, Sculpture, Architecture, and Drawing*

🏛 Antonio Canova

▼ *Psyche Revived by Cupid's Kiss, commissioned in 1787 and executed by Antonio Canova (1757–1822)*

The famous Neoclassical sculptor Antonio Canova worked for the Pope and for Napoleon's family. But his mythological-themed works are by far his best. Among them is the mesmerising *Psyche Revived by Cupid's Kiss*. In a Sleeping Beauty-like tale, Psyche falls into a deathlike state after inhaling some fumes from a flask she was asked to bring from the Underworld by Venus. The sculpture shows the moment when a winged Cupid, the god of love, revives Psyche with a kiss.

🏛 John Flaxman (1755–1826)

Another leading sculptor, Flaxman was also a designer, draughtsman, and engraver. He is famous for his work with Wedgewood's Jasperware, a popular type of stoneware that was perfected in 1775. Flaxman's designs were inspired by the forms of Ancient Rome. His 1808 monument to Admiral Nelson, a hero of the Napoleonic wars, is a Neoclassical masterpiece.

▶ *Hercules in the Garden of the Hesperides, designed by John Flaxman for Wedgewood, c. 1785*

Romanticism

The earliest examples of Romanticism can be seen in the works of the Spanish master El Greco (1541–1614). However, the style only took root towards the end of the 18th century. Romanticism took the heroic character of Neoclassicism, combined it with a revolutionary spirit, and expressed it with deep emotion. It was greatly inspired by poetry and literature. Artists of this genre held lofty beliefs in the goodness of humanity, justice for all, and a return to nature. They placed such feelings above reason and intellect. As a result, their art was a personal expression. It was an individual response to life, humanity, and the supernatural.

▲ The Nightmare, an eerie painting by Swiss artist Henry Fuseli (1741–1825), was one of the earliest works of Romanticism

▲ The 1827 Death of Sardanapalus by French Romantic artist Eugène Delacroix (1798–1863) was inspired by Lord Byron's popular play on the tragic last king of Assyria

 ## The Wanderer Above the Sea of Fog

The exceptionally talented Caspar David Friedrich (1774–1840) was a keen observer and painter of nature. He interpreted the natural world in deeply personal terms, reflecting a touch of the mysterious and the divine. His masterpiece of symbolism, *Wanderer Above the Sea of Fog,* shows a striking figure standing in contemplation at the top of a hill. Before him, the land is shrouded in a shifting fog. It is as if the man is mesmerised by his journey ahead, into an unknown future.

▲ Ossian Receiving the Ghosts of the French Heroes is a painting by early Romanticist Anne-Louis Girodet de Roussy, 1767–1824

▶ The Wanderer Above the Sea of Fog, c. 1818

Francisco Goya (1746–1828)

The Spanish artist Francisco José de Goya y Lucientes was a court painter to Charles III and Charles IV of Spain. A portrait artist and printmaker, he illustrated key historical events of the 18th and 19th centuries. His works are valued as an important part of pre-modern art. Some of Goya's most moving paintings are stamped with the violence that followed Napoleon's conquest of Spain. *The Third of May 1808* shows the execution of Spanish rebels who rose against the French troops. Its companion piece, *The Second of May 1808*, illustrates the actual uprising. This tribute to Spanish resistance has such emotional force, it is one of the lasting icons of anti-war art.

▲ *The Second of May 1808, also called The Charge of the Mamelukes, depicts the Spanish people's rebellion against the occupying forces of France during the Peninsular War*

▲ *The Third of May 1808 shows the merciless execution of Spanish rebels by Napoleon's soldiers*

The Lady of Shalott

The English artist John William Waterhouse (1849–1917) brought literary masterpieces to life with his marvellous paintings. His artworks are marked by broad brushstrokes and blocks of colour. Waterhouse's Romantic style was influenced by the Pre-Raphaelite movement, especially in his choice of subjects. This is seen in his most famous painting, *The Lady of Shalott*.

Painted in 1888, it illustrates Alfred Tennyson's famous poem of the same name, which is based on a legend from the time of King Arthur. The painting shows the tragic Elaine of Astolat, who defies a curse to go in search of her beloved knight. In her boat are three candles symbolising her life. Two of them have gone out, indicating the lady's fast approaching doom.

⭐ Incredible Individuals

In 1793, Goya suffered a serious illness that made him completely deaf. It left him somewhat isolated and prone to dark moods. This period marks a change in his paintings, which henceforth express a darker form of Romanticism.

◄ *Courtyard with Lunatics was painted in 1793–1794 at a time when Goya was turning deaf. He often heard voices in his head and worried that he was going mad*

◄ *This 1888 Lady of Shalott is the earliest and most evocative of Waterhouse's three beautiful paintings on the same subject*

Romanticism in Landscapes

Until the advent of Romanticism, landscapes were largely used as backgrounds for historical or heroic subjects. At best, they showed a sentimental country life. Such calm scenes came from biblical traditions and ideas. All this changed drastically in the hands of Romantic artists. Caspar David Friedrich, the founder of German Romantic landscape painting, believed that 'the artist should not only paint what he sees before him, but also what he sees in himself'. Thus, Romantic landscapes use the forces of nature to represent one's inner turmoil.

▲ Combining biblical subjects with sweeping sceneries, the English painter John Martin (1789–1854) produced sensational and apocalyptic landscapes, such as The Great Day of His Wrath (1853). Human beings are typically small in this genre of painting

▲ Gothic ruins made for magnificent landscapes, such as this Interior of Lindisfarne Priory (1797) by Thomas Girtin. Once again, the living beings are a minute part of a grander subject

 ## Trends in Landscape Painting

As attitudes towards landscape painting changed, artists began to portray wild, fluctuating sceneries, often with medieval buildings and ruins. This trend was first seen in English paintings from the latter half of the 18th century, with the works of such pioneers as Richard Wilson (1714–1782) and Thomas Girtin (1775–1802). Over the 19th century, different types of landscape art developed in the West. In Russia, it found expression through the *Peredvizhniki*, a group of artists nicknamed 'the Wanderers'. In America, the Hudson River School came to the forefront of landscape painting.

▲ The Rooks Have Come Back (1871), painted by Alexei Savrasov (1830–1897), a member of the Wanderers, when he was at the height of his career

▲ The stark yet sublime style of Richard Wilson, the father of English landscape painting, can be seen in his c. 1765 painting of the lake Llyn-y-Cau on the Cader Idris mountain in Wales

John Constable (1776–1837)

The son of a mill owner, John Constable grew up in an area of natural beauty. Blessed with keen observational powers, he expressed his appreciation of nature in evocative detail. Indeed, the Romantic painter Henry Fuseli once remarked that Constable's work 'makes me call for my greatcoat and umbrella'. Constable contributed greatly to English landscape painting, with such pieces as the incredibly lifelike painting *The Cornfield* (1826). This was inspired by James Thomson's poem *Summer*.

▶ *"A fresher gale begins to wave the woods and stir the streams, sweeping with shadowy gusts the fields of corn."—Summer, James Thomson*

 # The Hay Wain

One of Constable's most famous paintings, *The Hay Wain* (1821), was originally exhibited simply as *Landscape: Noon*. It captures the sunny, green nature of the English countryside in summer. It also represents the quiet contentment that Constable felt while surveying this familiar scene. The man in the painting is immersed in his surroundings, illustrating a Romantic belief of the relationship between nature and humanity.

▶ *The Hay Wain (1821) shows a scene on the River Stour and is one of Constable's most popular masterpieces*

 # The Battle of Trafalgar

Known as "the painter of light", John Mallord William Turner (1775–1851) is a celebrated master of English landscape painting. He had an entirely original way of mixing Romanticism and Realism, which inspired the spectacular Impressionist developments in landscape painting.

Unique among Turner's works is the *Battle of Trafalgar*. Under the command of Admiral Nelson, the battle established the supremacy of the English navy. Despite this victory, Turner's expression of military heroism focuses on chaos and death. The sea is turbulent with war. Ships clash and toss their men overboard. It shows the final moments of Admiral Nelson's tragic end.

◀ *The Battle of Trafalgar, painted 1822–1824*

The Pre-Raphaelites

Raphael was the most celebrated artist who lived and painted at the end of the Renaissance period. Over 300 years later, a group of British painters came together under his name. The founding members were three students of the Royal Academy of Arts—Dante Gabriel Rossetti, William Holman Hunt, and John Everett Millais. They were joined by others later on. Their aim was to return the arts to a time of higher inspiration. In 1848, the West was going through industrialisation. Photography was gaining popularity. The Pre-Raphaelites bemoaned the lack of imagination in the art of their times. Thus, they took inspiration from medieval sources like the legends of King Arthur, from Renaissance writers like Shakespeare, and from Romantic poets such as Keats.

▲ The Death of King Arthur, a tender medieval scene painted c. 1860 by James Archer (1823–1904)

▲ William Holman Hunt's 1868 painting titled Isabella and the Pot of Basil depicts a scene from a romantic and eerie poem by John Keats

 ## Marie Spartali (1844–1927)

Being an artist in Victorian England was not considered a 'suitable occupation' for a woman. Marie Spartali Stillman was one of the few professional female artists in the latter half of the 19th century. She was very successful and had close ties with the Pre-Raphaelite circle. Her 1885 watercolour *Love's Messenger* shows a woman standing by an open window. A dove has just delivered a letter into her hands. There are symbols of love all about her; the red rose on her dress, the blindfolded Cupid, and even the dove itself.

▶ Love's Messenger, by Marie Spartali Stillman, painted with symbols that express love and beauty in full bloom

Dante Gabriel Rossetti (1828–1882)

One of 19th century's most influential painters was Dante Gabriel Rossetti. A gifted poet, writer, translator, and artist, he was perhaps the most remarkable leader of the Pre-Raphaelite Brotherhood. His paintings were perhaps not skilled in a technical way, but they were so amazingly imaginative that you could not tear your eyes away from them. Many of the subjects were inspired by literature and were done in both oil and watercolours. Rossetti also created illustrations for stained glass windows like the scene of Tristram and Ysoude drinking a love potion in a legend from the time of King Arthur. One of Rossetti's most famous works is the *Beata Beatrix*, a deeply personal painting of his artist-wife Elizabeth Siddal painted in the years after her death.

▲ *Beata Beatrix (1864–1870) by Dante Gabriel Rossetti*

▲ *Sir Tristram and la Belle Ysoude drinking the love potion is a stained-glass window illustrated by Dante Gabriel Rossetti. It is part of a set of 13 stained glass panels, of which Rossetti designed two*

In Real Life

Dante Gabriel Rossetti's paintings are so popular, you can buy them online as poster art. He is best known to children today as the illustrator of the *Goblin Market*, a story in verse by his sister Christina Rossetti.

▶ *Sweet-toothed Laura pays for the goblin's wicked fruit with a lock of her golden hair, an illustration by Dante Gabriel Rossetti for the Goblin Market*

Isn't It Amazing!

Many famous people actually found the works of the Pre-Raphaelites irreverent and blasphemous. Key among them was the greatest novelist of the Victorian era, Charles Dickens.

▲ *John Everett Millais's brilliantly executed Christ in the House of His Parents (1849–1850) drew criticism from Charles Dickens, who thought the Virgin Mary had been depicted too hideously*

Realism

Originating in France in the 1850s, Realism aimed at illustrating objective truth. It did away with supernatural elements and artificial exaggerations. Exotic subjects and artistic traditions were discarded. Instead, Realists tried to show gritty, everyday facts. They held up a mirror to the industrial and commercial nature of their times. French Realism, as founded by Honoré Daumier, Jean-François Millet, and Gustave Courbet, honoured the working classes and their environment.

▲ The Birdcatcher, by Vasily Perov (1834–1882), who pioneered the new style of Critical Realism in Russian art

▲ Sad Inheritance (1899), by the Spanish artist Joaquín Sorolla y Bastida, is a striking painting of disabled children bathing in the sea. This style is known as Social Realism

The Realism Exhibition

The term Realism had been floating around since the 1840s, but it really took off after an incident in 1855. During the World's Fair in Paris, the painter Gustave Courbet was prevented from displaying one of his works titled *The Painter's Studio*. Not one to be discouraged by such rejection, Courbet set up his own exhibition. He sent out flyers and invited people to view his personal exhibition. It was called 'Pavilion of Realism'.

Courbet was inspired by Rembrandt's *The Night Watch* and *The Anatomy Lesson* to pursue Realism. His painting, *A Burial at Ornans,* shows the funeral of his great-uncle in his hometown. Rather than using models for the painting—as was considered normal—Courbet painted the very people who had been present at the burial. Critics thought he was making his pictures unnecessarily ugly; the subject of a large funeral was normally reserved for very important people.

◀ The Painter's Studio shows Courbet's friends, members of French society, and allegorical figures

The Third-Class Carriage

The railways were a miracle of the Industrial Age. They fascinated Honoré Daumier (1808–1879), who sketched and painted the realities of this new mode of transportation. In *The Third-Class Carriage*, Daumier observes the cramped, dirty compartments that working-class Parisians were forced to travel in. He paints with sympathy, a family of women and children in the front row. The whole scene captures the plight of the people and a moment of quiet in their harried lives.

▲ *The Third-Class Carriage, c. 1862–1864, by Daumier*

The Gross Clinic

One of the best American Realist paintings ever created is *The Clinic of Dr Gross*, an 1875 masterpiece by the painter, photographer, and sculptor Thomas Eakins. The painting illustrates a lecture in modern surgery, given by the famous Philadelphia surgeon Dr Samuel Gross. Eakins paints this pioneering medical man in a severe yet heroic manner. He is upright, his forehead glows, and the blood on his hands catches the light as he pauses to explain the procedure.

▲ *The Gross Clinic (1875) by Thomas Eakins*

Next to him, the mother of the patient covers her face in horror. The assistants are engrossed in the surgery. When the painting was exhibited, people did not know how to react. Indeed, the viewers may have found it morbid and criticised the artist, judging the detail to be too realistic. The work was even rejected by the Centennial Exhibition of 1876. Today, it is one of the most celebrated paintings in its genre.

▶ *Incense of a New Church (1921), by Charles Demuth (1883–1935), demonstrates the Precisionist style. Sharp industrial smog and dark factories replaced the churches that once dominated the American landscape*

In Real Life

Courbet's painting *The Stonebreakers* (1849) is a sympathetic work showing the artist's concern for the difficulties of the poor. The canvas shows two men toiling under the sun, breaking and removing stones from a road that is under construction. The painting was destroyed in the bombing of Germany in WWII.

▲ *The Stonebreakers (1849) by Gustave Courbet*

Realism in the 20th Century

With a series of horrific wars, the **Great Depression** and the development of nuclear weapons, 20th century Realists had a plethora of subjects to choose from. Modern Realism thus, split into a wide variety of forms. For instance, the 1920s saw the rise of Precisionism in America. This style captured urban landscapes in sharp-focus realism.

Impressionism

During the late 1860s and early 1870s, Paris (and then France) saw the rise of Impressionism. This became one of the most influential pre-modern art movements. The name was coined in 1874 by Louis Leroy, a French art critic, after he saw Claude Monet's 1872 painting titled *Impression: Sunrise*. In its purest form, Impressionism advocates *plein-air* painting, which means painting outdoors. It is identified by rapid, loose brushstrokes, and the spontaneous application of paint. Impressionists tried to capture fleeting moments in light. A landscape that turned orange in the sunset would be painted orange. This non-natural depiction of light and swift brushwork made Impressionism a revolutionary movement in Western art.

▲ *Impression, soleil levant (in English, Sunrise) by Claude Monet (1840–1926), one of the founders and most prolific artists of Impressionism*

🏛 Camille Pissarro (1830–1903)

A father figure to many artists of his time, Camille Pissarro sought to depict nature in its myriad colours and changing tones. He was central to the Impressionist and Post-Impressionist movements and was often treated as a mentor and teacher. His first paintings in the genre shocked people. They were regarded as too muddy and too rustic. People were more used to heroic and mythological subjects. Pissarro's ways of using colour to show shadows and light was also considered revolutionary.

🏛 Alfred Sisley (1839–1899)

The 'forgotten Impressionist', Alfred Sisley was a master of *plein-air* painting. A skilled yet underestimated Impressionist, he painted natural landscapes. Though he was a British citizen, he spent most of his time in France capturing its countryside and waterways in open compositions and vivid colours. His work differs from other Impressionists in its thoughtful and balanced composition, and a gentle quietness that permeates each canvas.

▲ *Pont Boieldieu in Rouen, Rainy Weather is an 1896 painting by Pissarro of a new iron bridge near the Gare d'Orléans train station and the Place Carnot square. Here, Pissarro moved beyond traditional rural landscapes to a busy industrial area; eventually depicting it in a number of paintings under different light and weather conditions*

▲ *The Terrace at Saint-Germain, Spring (1875) by Alfred Sisely*

Édouard Manet (1832–1883)

Related to the French monarch, Manet was highly revered by Impressionist painters. By the age of 29, the precocious artist was already considered the movement's leading figure. Manet's mesmerising paintings captured the dynamic city life of Paris and the leisurely pastimes of its upper class. He painted bars, cafes, clubs, and races. He was also a noted portrait artist, reflecting the joys and the loneliness of urban people.

▲ An early painting, the 1862 Music in the Tuileries Gardens shows a fashionable crowd gathered at the famous Paris gardens for a concert. The painting includes portraits of Manet's friends and family

Edgar Degas (1834–1917)

Famous for his many, many paintings of ballet dancers, Edgar Degas was less focused on the effects of light and more interested in natural gestures and movements. His carefully balanced works offer a snapshot of his subjects' unguarded moments. Unlike other artists of Impressionism, he rarely attempted *plein-air* painting. Instead, he preferred to work at his studio producing amazing artworks with watercolours, sketches, pastels, and sculptures.

▲ Degas's ballet dancers seem poised to dance right out of the canvas

Paul Cézanne (1839–1906)

An important artist of Impressionism and Post-Impressionism, the French painter Paul Cézanne is revered as the "father of modern art". His developments in colour, composition, and perspective led the transition to 20th century art. His works are easily identified by their repetitive brushwork. The genius Pablo Picasso acknowledged him as "my one and only master".

▲ One of the five paintings in the series titled The Card Players, which marked the start of Cézanne's greatest period of art

Pierre-Auguste Renoir (1841–1919)

A master at portraying 'dappled light', Renoir was a genius painter of women, children, and nature. His *plein-air* painting vividly captures shifting lights. His earlier works are marked by dark colours and the heavy technique called **impasto**. After 1868, his colours became lighter and more natural. This was in part due to his work with fellow artist Monet.

▲ The Dance at Le Moulin de la Galette (1876), shows Renoir's incredible depiction of dappled afternoon light playing over the faces and clothes of the festive people

Post-Impressionist Art

Post-Impressionism is the general style of art that appeared during the 1880s and the 1890s. It was pioneered by the generation of artists who followed the Impressionists. They were not content with being restricted to nature and *plein-air* painting. They experimented widely with colour. The period saw the rise of many art movements such as Neo-Impressionism, early Expressionism, and Fauvism.

Whistler's Mother

The 1871 *Arrangement in Grey and Black No.1* is an iconic American painting popularly called *Whistler's Mother*. It is a portrait of Anna Matilda, the devout, strict mother of James Abbott McNeill Whistler (1834–1903). According to legend, she posed for this painting when one of Whistler's sitters failed to turn up. The artist, who avoided morality and sentimentality in his work (which is apparent from the title), painted Anna in austere shades. The brilliance of the work lies in its carefully balanced composition and shapes.

▶ *Arrangement in Grey and Black No.1 by James Whistler*

Neo-Impressionists

The **avant-garde** Neo-Impressionists refined the impulsive Impressionist movement with a special way of painting. Instead of mixing colours on a **palette** and applying it to the canvas, Neo-Impressionists dotted their colours directly on to the canvas. These groups of coloured points formed a coherent image in the mind of the viewer. This method is called Pointillist painting. It gives greater luminescence to pigments and a brilliance to the whole piece. Neo-Impressionism was founded by Georges Seurat (1859–1891) and his disciple Paul Signac (1863–1935).

Seurat's Pointillism

A Sunday Afternoon on the Island of La Grande Jatte (1884–1886) is the Georges Seurat masterpiece that kicked off the Neo-Impressionist movement. Look closely and you will notice the whole painting is a series of closely packed dots. Seurat went to the park every day at the same hour for months. He sketched the visitors, went back to his studio and transferred his observations onto the canvas. The people thus, seem isolated and silent.

◀ *A Sunday Afternoon on the Island of La Grande Jatte (1884–1886) by Seurat*

Paul Signac

After the death of Seurat, the Post-Impressionist painter Paul Signac became the leader of the Neo-Impressionist art movement. Signac's work largely comprises vividly coloured landscapes and seascapes. He further developed Seurat's Pointillism. His experiments with different ways of applying colour influenced later schools of art, including Fauvism. His greatest pieces include *The Papal Palace, Avignon* (1900), and *Port of Marseilles* (1905).

Fauvism

A short-lived art movement, the highly fashionable Fauvism, was associated with a group of French artists between 1905 and 1907. Henri Matisse (1869–1954) and André Derain (1880–1954) were the leaders of this style. The word comes from the French term *les fauves*, meaning "the wild beasts". The style was characterised by wild brushwork, contrasting colours, and simplified figures. People were shocked by the paintings at first because they were unlike anything ever seen in the art world.

▲ *The Port of Saint-Tropez (1901–1902) by Paul Signac*

Japonism

Many French Impressionists and Post-Impressionists, from Monet to Vincent van Gogh, were influenced by Japanese art trends, especially by the woodblock prints of c.1600–1900 termed *ukiyo-e* (pictures of the floating world). The most influential works came from Hokusai (1760–1849) and Hiroshige (1797–1858).

▲ *Under the Wave off Kanagawa, c. 1830–1832, the most famous of Hokusai's prints, is the first of a series called Thirty-six Views of Mount Fuji. Notice the snow-clad mountain in the distance*

▲ *Vivid expressions using bright, unnatural colours mark the short-lived Fauvist style*

💡 Isn't It Amazing!

In 1885, the song-writing duo Gilbert and Sullivan lampooned British traditions and government in a comic opera set in fictional Japan. *The Mikado* has remained popular ever since.

▶ *The 1885 poster announcing The Mikado shows its three heroines— Yum-Yum, Pitti-Sing, and Peep-Bo*

Van Gogh (1853–1890)

One of the most celebrated Post-Impressionists in the world today is the Dutch painter Vincent van Gogh. Van Gogh only painted during the last decade of his short life. But these proved to be prolific years, with the artist creating a new picture almost every four days. His energetic, almost frantic paintings reflected his life, and state of mind. From his vivid self-portraits, to the enthusiastically bright *Sunflowers* and many ominous landscapes, the paintings reflected the artist's days, the influence of his friends, his intense inner world, and his fading health.

▲ Van Gogh was influenced by Japanese art, as seen here in his 1887 oil painting The Courtesan (after Eisen). This specifically refers to the work of Japanese artist Kesai Eisen

▲ It is generally believed that Vincent sold only one painting during his lifetime—The Red Vineyard, painted in 1888 near Arles, France

🏛 The Early Style

Vincent first began drawing with pencils, charcoal sticks and watercolours. His early subjects were poor, hardworking people for whom he felt great sympathy. His early oil paintings also show similar subjects in dark, gritty colours. Most famous among them is *The Potato Eaters* (1885). This grim picture shows a peasant family at their frugal dinner. Their coarse and ugly faces were the result of several studies by van Gogh. However, most of his contemporaries were displeased with the unflattering realities it portrayed.

◀ The Potato Eaters (1885)

⊙ Incredible Individuals

As a young man, Vincent tried and failed at numerous jobs. He was a teacher, a minister, worked at a bookstore, an art gallery, and even became a missionary. He finally dedicated his life to art around the age of 27. He was supported by his brother Theo, who sent him money, encouragement, and even tried (unsuccessfully) to sell his paintings.

▶ Worn Out, an 1882 pencil sketch of a war veteran at a local almshouse

The Maturing Painter

Van Gogh moved to Paris in 1886 to live with his brother Theo and learn from the artists. Here, he was influenced by men such as Monet, Degas, Pissarro, and even became friends with Gauguin. Vincent learned to use bright colours and new techniques of brushwork. He practiced making portraits—even painting 20 self-portraits when he could find no other models!

In 1888, he found a house in Arles in sunny southern France, where he painted his vibrant, happy *Sunflowers* series. Van Gogh's paintings took on new intensity and emotion here. Not only did he choose more vibrant colours, he often applied paint directly from the tube to the canvas. He painted with such thick rough brush strokes that the paintings would take weeks to dry.

▶ *After a heated confrontation with Paul Gauguin, during a mental breakdown, van Gogh cut off part of his left ear, wrapped it up and gave it to a woman for safekeeping. He later painted a self-portrait with his bandaged ear*

▲ *Vase of Twelve Sunflowers (1888), part of a series painted in Arles. The second painting of the series was part of a Japanese collection and was destroyed in a fire during WWII*

 ## Fading Health

By 1889, van Gogh had become so moody, depressed and unpredictable, he committed himself to a mental hospital. He was no longer able to look after himself. Yet, he painted with vigour. Some of his most enduring works like the exquisite *Starry Night,* with its cypress trees and swirling colours, come from this period. In July 1890, he committed suicide by shooting himself in the chest.

▶ *Van Gogh's mesmerising, swirling Starry Night illustrates a moonlit scene near the asylum where he stayed*

▲ *Wheatfield with Crows (1890), often thought to be van Gogh's greatest and last artwork*

Symbolism

A late 19ᵗʰ century Post-Impressionist movement, Symbolism flourished throughout Europe, particularly in German, French, and Belgian regions. It arose in literature and poetry and soon spread to other art forms. Symbolism had deep connections with the Pre-Raphaelites and Romanticism. In turn, it influenced Expressionism and Surrealism. Symbolism came about as a reaction against Realism and its gritty, objective focus. Instead, Symbolists chose mythological and fantastical subjects. They looked for the extraordinary. They searched for a deeper reality arising from their dreams and inner world.

▲ At the height of his Golden Period, Austrian artist Gustav Klimt painted The Kiss an oil painting covered in gold and silver leaf to symbolise the wonderfulness of love

Death of the Gravedigger

This lovely painting by the German painter Carlos Schwabe (1866–1926) is full of Symbolist motifs. The painting features a gravedigger digging his own grave, while the angel of death visits him. The gravedigger's face is peaceful even in death, while his soul (the green light) is taken away in the protective arms of the angel.

▲ 'The Knight at the Crossroads' (1882) by Victor Vasnetsov brings to life a Russian legend, The Three Journeys of Ilya Muromets. On a bleak landscape, the hero pauses over this stone inscription: 'If you go straight ahead, there will be no life; there is no way forward for he who travels past, walks past, or flies past'.

In Real Life

In 1989, Chinese troops gunned down students and civilians who were protesting for democracy at the Tiananmen Square in Beijing. This shocking massacre and the uncertain times that followed gave birth to protest paintings in a style called Cynical Realism. Chinese painters used Symbolist motifs to convey their message of irony and ridicule.

▲ Death of the Gravedigger (1895) by German painter Carlos Schwabe (1866–1926)

The Lady with the Pig

The best-known work of Félicien Rops (1833–1898), a Belgian artist and pioneer of Belgian comics, is titled *Pornocrates or The Lady with the Pig*. The pig here symbolises luxury and evil. It is misleading a woman, who follows with a blindfold over her eyes. They stand on a marble stage, below which are allegorical male figures of the arts like Sculpture, Music, Poetry and Painting. The fine arts seem to despair beneath the heels of decadence.

The Flying Carpet

One of the first artists to turn fantasies into paintings, Viktor Mikhaylovich Vasnetsov (1848–1926) caused a media storm with his *The Flying Carpet*. In this fairy tale picture, he expressed the Russian people's longing for a bright future. The hero soars freely in the bright open sky. He stands confidently, richly clothed, holding magical gifts like the large golden cage of a firebird. The carpet—an amazing vehicle—was also drawn for the sake of Savva Mamontov, the wealthy industrialist who commissioned the painting.

▲ *The Flying Carpet is Vasnetsov's 1880 depiction of Ivan Tsarevich, a hero from Russian folktales*

⊛ Incredible Individuals

One of the giants of Post-Impressionist Symbolism was the enigmatic painter Paul Gauguin (1848–1903). He developed a simplified, non-naturalistic style of painting to express his emotions. This is recognisable in his decorative line work, flat bold colours, and perplexing use of symbols. Tragically, few people appreciated his works while he was alive, and he died in poverty.

▲ *Gauguin's 1897–1898 painting titled Where Do We Come From? What Are We? Where Are We Going?*

RENAISSANCE ARCHITECTURE

BUILDINGS OF THE RENAISSANCE

Beginning from the 14th century, architects in the Italian states began to revive Classical Roman and Greek designs for buildings. The new designs became part of the period called the **Renaissance**. Classicism stressed the importance of harmony, symmetry and proportion in all structures, whether a single building or an entire city. The earliest masters of the Renaissance period, like Filippo Brunelleschi, rose in Florence. He was an architect and an engineer. Some of his constructions used machines that he had invented himself. During the **High Renaissance**, the focus shifted to Rome and to geniuses like Donato Bramante, an architect who served as the chief architect for the construction of St. Peter's Basilica. During the 15th and 16th centuries, the Renaissance spread to the rest of Europe. Here, it combined with native styles to produce entirely unique buildings.

▼ The Duomo di Firenze (Cathedral of Florence) is famous for its Renaissance dome. It was built by the architect Filippo Brunelleschi who invented new ways of engineering to make such a construction possible

Identifying Renaissance Architecture

Renaissance architecture was inspired by Classical notions of order. This can be seen in the geometrical layouts of buildings. Rows of columns and round arches were often repeated in tiers. Proportions (its size and symmetry) were designed according to certain Classical and mathematical formulae. They matched human proportions, the Renaissance ideal of beauty and harmony. Renaissance architects also looked to ancient Roman architects like Vitruvius to guide them in designing the ideal building.

▲ Designed by early Renaissance master Leon Battista Alberti, the amazing facade of the Basilica of Sant'Andrea in Mantua reflects Classical Roman grandeur

▲ The Palazzo Mellini-Fossi of Florence is unusual for having frescoes on the outside rather than its interior. This Renaissance building is painted with scenes from Roman mythology

▲ The Baptistery of Florence is an early revival of Classical symmetry; the blind arches are typical of Renaissance decoration

 ## Renaissance Motifs

Architects of the Renaissance rejected the ornate designs of the earlier Gothic period. On the outside, buildings were relatively flat and plain. Their beauty came from the marble or stone used in construction and from the repetitions of set geometrical patterns. Ancient motifs seen here included blind arches, medallions and three types of Classical columns—Doric, Ionic, and Corinthian. Statues were used to decorate nooks and rooftops.

The most easily recognisable order of architecture, Doric is characterised by columns topped by plain circular capitals. The Ionic column is topped by two pairs of volutes. This is a spiral, scroll-like ornament for the pillar. Ionic columns are usually slender and were considered 'female' during Renaissance times. The most complex decoration of columns is called Corinthian. It is seen both on the facades of and insides of buildings, where it adds vigour to otherwise strictly Classical lines. The Corinthian pillars end in unfurling leaf and fern-like motifs. Later, composite columns were created, combining Corinthian columns with Doric or Ionic orders to create designs that were even more ornate.

▲ This Renaissance Puerta del Puente (Gate of the Bridge) has a central square passage with sturdy Doric columns on either side

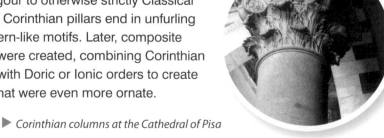

▶ Corinthian columns at the Cathedral of Pisa

▲ The volutes atop Ionic columns at Palazzo Valmarana

Sansovino's Biblioteca

Jacopo Sansovino (1486–1570) brought the High Renaissance style of architecture to Venice. The library that he designed at Piazza San Marco (St. Mark's Square) features regular **bays** in endlessly repeating rows. The space between the arches is decorated with Classical figures and motifs. On the rooftop are tall, elegant statues that offer a vertical contrast to the long building.

▶ *Sansovino's Biblioteca Marciana inspired many later Renaissance architects*

 ## Urban Planning

Renaissance architecture went hand in hand with town planning. It first began with Florence. Unlike other towns of the 15th century, Florence was not dominated by cathedral spires rising above smaller houses and churches. Instead, it was planned to radiate away from the centre in the shape of a star. This model was considered the Classical ideal and was much imitated. The buildings on each street were well defined and created according to harmonious proportions.

▲ *The Ideal City, painted c. 1480–1484, shows the ideal Renaissance town with its triumphant archway, Roman colosseum and octagonal baptistery surrounded by dignified homes. The entire space is broken up according to mathematical principles and reflects a harmony of proportions*

 ## Old Town of Urbino

The hill town of Urbino was a flourishing centre of Renaissance in the 15th century. Under the patronage of its military leader Federico da Montefeltro (1422–1482), the city became a centre for the arts. The architects who were attracted to the city built it according to Renaissance traditions. The University of Urbino, set up in 1506, still operates today. However, from the 16th century onwards, the town's culture and economy began to decline. It has thus preserved its Renaissance appearance and is now a UNESCO World Heritage Site.

▶ *The historic centre of Urbino*

Early Renaissance in Florence

Florence began as an ancient Roman garrison town.
During the Renaissance, however, it transformed into a
prosperous town of merchants and scholars. The artists
and architects who flocked here transformed the city
with fine Classical buildings and sculptures.

▶ *The facade of Santa Maria Novella, completed in
1470 by influential architect Leon Battista Alberti, in
a mix of Gothic and Renaissance styles*

 ## Baptistery Doors

The eastern doors of the Baptistery of San Giovanni are part of
Renaissance legend. Created by Lorenzo Ghiberti (1378–1455),
the doors are so extraordinary, Michelangelo named them the
'Gates of Paradise'. They are about 17 ft tall. Each side is divided
into five square panels, bearing stories in **relief** from the Old
Testament. Inspiration for the figures came from ancient Roman
sarcophagus reliefs. The frame of each door is ornamented with
statuettes and **roundels**. At the very top and bottom, the frames
bear reclining figures.

▶ *The Gates of Paradise at the Florence Baptistery*

The Gates of Paradise

Ghiberti won the commission to create the doors by beating
amazing competitors such as architect Filippo Brunelleschi
and sculptor Niccolo d'Arezzo. It took ten years to complete
just the door panels. Work on the frames went on till the 1440s.
Finally, in 1452, the gilding of the doors was completed. The
doors were fixed at the Baptistery's eastern entrance, and
Ghiberti died three years later.

▲ *This door panel shows God creating the universe,
the Garden of Eden and the first humans*

▲ *The panel depicting the life of Joshua, who led the
Israelites after the death of Moses*

▲ *One of the roundels bears
a self-portrait of Ghiberti*

Pazzi Chapel

One of Filippo Brunelleschi's masterpieces, the Pazzi Chapel follows a circle-and-square design. The atrium, which is a kind of entrance hall, is held up by six Corinthian columns. Inside, the square room lies below an umbrella-shaped dome, bearing round sculptures and the Pazzi coat-of-arms. The walls carry glazed terracotta decorations by Luca della Robbia. The vault over the **apse** is frescoed to reflect the sky over Florence on 4 July 1442.

▲ Luca della Robbia's decorations inside the Pazzi Chapel, with the sky-dome beyond the arch

In Real Life

In 1478, Jacopo and Francesco de Pazzi ambushed their rivals in the Medici family and murdered one of them. The Pazzis paid dearly for their crime. They were exiled and all their lands were confiscated. As a result, the Pazzi Chapel you see today is still left unfinished.

▶ A 1479 drawing of a hanged Pazzi conspirator by Leonardo da Vinci

Palazzo Medici-Riccardi

Around 1444, Cosimo de' Medici hired the architect Michelozzo to build him a home. This became Florence's first Renaissance palatial townhouse. From outside, it is as stern and formidable as a fortress. The rows of arched windows and asymmetrical doors offer little relief. In 1517, the ground floor was altered by adding two 'kneeling windows' designed by Michelangelo. The internal courtyard is a far gentler space. It lies between arched colonnades. A staircase leads to the various quarters and their amazing frescoes.

▲ Michelangelo's 'kneeling window' (finestre inginocchiate) at the Palazzo Medici-Riccardi

▲ The inner courtyard is decorated with the statue of Greek mythological hero Orpheus at the far end

Palazzo Strozzi

The Strozzi family were rivals of the Medicis in Florence. The Palazzo Strozzi was thus purposely designed to be bigger and better than the Palazzo Medici-Riccardi. Work began in 1489 using a design by Benedetto da Maiano. But later, the architect Simone del Pollaiolo took over. This is yet another fortress-like residence. It is built in a rectangle and occupies three floors. A symmetrical structure, it is made of massive stone blocks. Wrought-iron decorations such as torch-holders and flag-holders adorn the facade. The courtyard is surrounded by a stone arcade.

▶ At Palazzo Strozzi, wrought-iron decorations in the shapes of a sphinx and dragon created by the 15th century blacksmith Niccolò Grosso

Domes on the Skyline

Domed roofs have been around since ancient times. But it was only in Roman times that they became technical marvels. Ancient Roman architects developed engineering principles to build impressive domes. Their knowledge was revived and further developed during the Renaissance. The dome became an architectural wonder. It crowned the most important, most imposing buildings of the Renaissance.

◀ The double domes of Santa Maria della Salute, on the Grand Canal of Venice, evolved from the revival and further development of ancient Roman styles and engineering. The church was built to thank God for saving the city from the devastating plague outbreak of 1630

An Architectural Challenge

Domes exert all their pressure outwards along the boundary and can easily collapse. Renaissance builders who planned ambitious domes came up with ways to reduce the weight and pressure of the stone. For instance, they used a system of ribs to support the structure during construction. Such techniques allowed for great variation in the curve and high, awe-inspiring **drums**. Many domes even had a second, lighter shell on the inside that made the outside and the inside look very different.

▲ The dome at Prato's Santa Maria delle Carceri, designed by architect Giuliano da Sangallo, was inspired by Brunelleschi's work. While the inside is a perfect half-sphere, the outside is a combination of cylindrical and conical shapes

The Duomo

The amazing dome of the Cathedral Santa Maria del Fiore began an architectural revolution. This cathedral in Florence is also known as the Duomo. Its construction began in 1296. In 1418, a competition was held to decide who would construct the dome for the cathedral. It was to be almost 150 feet wide, a very difficult feat. After much discussion, Filippo Brunelleschi finally won the competition in 1420. The work on the dome began the same year and finally concluded in 1436.

▲ Florence's Duomo seen from Michelangelo Hill

⊛ Incredible Individuals

A talented architect, Filippo Brunelleschi (1377–1446) presented keen technical knowledge and amazing innovations, which marked the beginning of Renaissance architecture. The Duomo, his masterpiece, is the first octagonal dome in history. Brunelleschi designed it with a lantern crowning the top and tribunes (semicircular structures) down the side. He even invented the machines that helped construct the dome! Brunelleschi became the *capomaestro* (chief architect) from 1420 until his death in 1446.

Brunelleschi's Dome

Brunelleschi began constructing the dome by first building a tall drum, that is, a cylindrical base. His revolutionary bit of engineering called for a double-shelled dome of brick and stone. Using a wooden frame, the brickwork was placed in a herringbone pattern between stone beams. The octagonal outer shell grew into a pointed arch, supported by ribs. At the very top was an opening topped by a lantern. The inner and outer shells of the dome were held together by a system of arches. In the end, this unit was a freestanding dome requiring no external support!

▶ *Giorgio Vasari and Federico Zuccaro painted the inside of Brunelleschi's dome with frescoes of the Last Judgement*

St. Peter's Basilica

Brilliant architects like Bramante, Raphael, and Antonio da Sangallo helped build St. Peter's Basilica in Vatican City. Its dome (42 metre in diameter) was designed by Michelangelo using Brunelleschi's methods. It had two shells of wood and stone. When Michelangelo passed away in 1564, Giacomo della Porta completed the work using Michelangelo's basic design. This was a segmented dome with regularly spaced openings. The whole structure rested on a high drum, which had its own windows between paired columns. At the top was a tall and exquisite lantern. Della Porta made the dome higher, gave it more segments, and changed the shape of the openings.

▲ *The inner dome of St. Peter's Basilica, Vatican City*

▶ *The amazing High Renaissance dome at St. Peter's Basilica*

A Patrician's Home is His Palazzo

In Renaissance Italy, grand city homes were called palazzi (palazzo in singular). These were not always owned by noblemen. In fact, most palazzi belonged to wealthy **burghers** and clergymen. In general, they were sturdy, rectangular buildings that rose to three or more floors. They had formidable exteriors built to Classical proportions. Later in the Renaissance period, the buildings became more ornate.

▲ The late-Renaissance Palazzo Chiericati, designed by Andrea Palladio, has a more ornamental facade but still follows Classical principles in its construction

▲ Palazzo Marino, an ambitious High Renaissance townhouse designed by Galeazzo Alessi for the powerful banker Tommaso Marino. It is now Milan's city hall

 Palazzo Interiors

Sumptuous courtyards and walled gardens lay inside a palazzo, decorated with brilliant sculptures and fragrant plants. The rooms were vibrantly frescoed by the masters of the period.

▲ The amazing Sala dei Fasti Farnesiani (Room of Farnese Deeds) at Villa Farnese is the work of brothers Taddeo and Federico Zuccaro. They depicted the glorious history of the Farnese family

 Villa Farnese

The Villa Farnese dominates the town of Caprarola. It is an amazing Renaissance and Mannerist building that overlooks the hills of Monti Cimini. The palazzo is built in the form of a pentagon in reddish-gold stone. Antonio da Sangallo the Younger (1484–1546), a brilliant military engineer, originally designed it as a five-sided fortress. In the mid 16th century, architect Giacomo Barozzi da Vignola (1507–1573) took over. He kept the shape but created a grand palazzo with hundreds of rooms and a beautiful garden.

▼ An example of Renaissance architecture, Villa Farnese is large and built using harmonious proportions, but is sparingly ornamented

Royal Stairs

Supported by Ionic columns, Villa Farnese's galleried court is ornamented with busts of the Roman emperors. Five spiral staircases lead to the upper floors. The most magnificent of these is a graceful spiral of steps called the *Scala Regia* (Royal Stairs). It is held up by Ionic pillars and rises up three magnificent floors.

▲ *The upper landing of the Scala Regia*

▲ *View of the dome from the Scala Regia*

Hall of Hercules

Each of the five floors at Villa Farnese has a different purpose. The main rooms are on the *piano nobile* (first floor). Here, a central **loggia** looks down over the town. This hall is called the Sala d'Ercole (Hall of Hercules), after its mythological frescoes done by Federico Zuccaro (c. 1541–1609). At one end is a grotto-like fountain with statues.

▶ *The fountain in the Hall of Hercules*

Palazzo del Te

The summer palace of Duke Federico Gonzaga II, Palazzo del Te was built over c.1525–1535 by Giulio Romano. Not only did he work on the very building itself, Romano—a skilled designer and artist—worked hard and long at decorating the palatial interiors. He created illusions using form, texture and colour. Romano's many skills and incredible imagination led to the wonderful garden grottoes and mesmerising frescoes at the Palazzo del Te. Both the palace and its frescoes are important works of the Mannerist movement.

▲ *Wedding Banquet of Cupid and Psyche, a fresco by Giulio Romano at Palazzo del Te*

▲ *Detail from the Fall of the Giants shows Romano's skill at turning a flat wall into a brilliant and turbulent 3D illusion*

A Vista of Villas

Villas are grand country estates. They were first built as rambling homes for wealthy Romans in ancient times. The better-preserved ruins of such villas inspired Renaissance architects in the 15th and 16th centuries. This influence can be seen in the Villa Madama designed by Raphael. Ancient villas also influenced Pope Pius IV's Casino, built by Pirro Ligorio, in the Vatican gardens. However, Renaissance villas tried to be more symmetrical and less rambling. The first villas were built by the affluent Medici family. A symbol of power, villas were adorned with long colonnades, towers, and gardens. Water features were incredibly popular and gardens featured fountains, reflecting pools, and large reservoirs.

▲ Fontana dell'Ovato at the Villa d'Este

▲ Villa Barbaro, one of many iconic villas created by Andrea Palladio, is now a UNESCO World Heritage Site

▲ The magnificent Villa Aldobrandini, designed by Giacomo della Porta

Medici Villas

The Medici family constructed several villas in their home state of Tuscany. Many of these villas are now UNESCO World Heritage Sites. The villas were both leisure homes and palaces from which the Medicis ruled the land. One of the oldest is Cafaggiolo Castle. In 1443, Cosimo the Elder asked the architect Michelozzo to turn the castle into a villa. It is now a masterpiece of Renaissance architecture.

Equally old is the villa at Careggi. Like most Florentine villas, it is also a working farm. Michelozzo remodelled the fortified villa. He opened it up by building loggias. Those on the upper floor looked out over a walled garden full of myrtles, olives, oaks, poplars, pines and citrus trees. Other such early villas came about from the extensive rebuilding of older Medici castles.

▲ Medici Villa di Cafaggiolo

▶ A view of the Villa di Cafaggiolo painted by 16th century Flemish artist Giusto Utens

▲ Villa Medici at Careggi

Villa Medici in Fiesole

Michelozzo built the Villa Medici in Fiesole from scratch. Thus, it has a stronger Renaissance character. The villa became a gathering place for artists and scholars. Michelozzo had followed Classical ideals in his design. The villa is a quadrangular building with square stone windows and broad loggias. Built over 1451–1457, this Medici villa has elegant terraces cut into a stony hillside. There are broad and amazing views of the River Arno and the city of Florence.

▶ *Villa Medici at Fiesole*

Villa d'Este

The fabulous Villa d'Este is an estate in Tivoli with Mannerist buildings, grand fountains, and terraced gardens. The architect Pirro Ligorio created it for Cardinal Ippolito II d'Este. The villa is most famous for its mid 16th century gardens, set on a steep slope of the Sabine hills. A river plunges down the slope and its waters are channelled into a wonderful variety of fountains, including the remarkable 'water organ'. The stream runs around the garden ostentatiously creating a forceful, theatrical effect.

▲ *Water rising from the Villa d'Este's Fountain of Neptune, with the famous water organ in the background*

▲ *Pegasus in the gardens of Villa d'Este*

💡 Isn't It Amazing!

Ligorio's design for Villa d'Este was influenced by Roman ruins in Tivoli. The town of Tivoli had long been a popular summer residence due to its cool, high location, and its closeness to the villa of the ancient Roman Emperor Hadrian I. In fact, statues dug up from the ancient villa ultimately decorated the gardens of the Cardinal's villa.

Secular Architecture

Renaissance architects aligned themselves with Humanism, in which humanity and individuality are of more importance than dogma and superstition. As a result, architects of the time had great civic pride. This led to the construction of many secular buildings for public prosperity. One of the first was Brunelleschi's Hospital of the Innocents, an orphanage, with its elegant colonnade linking the charitable home to the public square. Another was the Laurentian Library where scholars could consult the immense collection of books established by the Medici family. The spirit of individuality eventually led many Renaissance architects to Mannerism. This broke through the strict regularity and mathematical proportions of Roman times to more playful and exaggerated symmetries.

▲ Frescoes such as the 1610 Visit of Cosimo II de Medici in the Foundling Hospital by Bernardo Poccetti adorn the Renaissance orphanage Ospedale degli Innocenti (Hospital of the Innocents)

 ## Teatro Olimpico

Built by the genius Andrea Palladio, the Teatro Olimpico is the only surviving theatre of its time. It was also the first indoor theatre built using stone. This is because, during the Renaissance, a theatre was not a standalone building. It was more of a temporary arrangement in a courtyard or a hall. The Teatro Olimpico's design was based on the ancient Roman theatre at Orange, France. The stage is 25 metres across and 7 metres deep. It looks up to steep tiers of seats. Palladio's theatre sits inside a pre-existing hall. Although it is indoors, it creates the illusion of being outside! The ceiling is painted sky blue. Additionally, it has the most elaborate *scaenae frons*—which is the decorated and permanent background of a Roman theatre—It has five doors. Beyond the large central door are three different vistas of city streets. Behind the four other doors are forced perspective views of a city street.

▲ The stage at Teatro Olimpico; the scaenae frons beyond the central door was done in wood and plaster by the famous architect and stage designer Vincenzo Scamozzi (1552–1616)

▲ Teatro Olimpico with its statue-filled niches and blue sky ceiling

Bridge of Sighs

The Ponte dei Sospiri (Bridge of Sighs) is a landmark of Venice. It is an arched, fully enclosed structure of white limestone. Built in 1600, it runs over a narrow canal between the Doge's Palace and the prisons. Antonio Contino designed this bridge with a single arch and in Istrian stone. The two barred windows offered passing convicts their last look at the world before they were imprisoned. Their supposed sighs gave the bridge its name. The top of the bridge is decorated with scrolls. At the bottom, a series of stern faces look down on passing gondolas.

▲ *Gondolas row past the grim heads of the Bridge of Sighs, Venice*

Laurentian Library

In 1523, Michelangelo was asked to build a library for the Medicis' extensive collection of books and manuscripts. The resulting Laurentian Library sits on the third storey atop older monastic buildings. It is made up of a reading room and a vestibule (entrance hall). The vestibule is one of Michelangelo's great achievements. It is famous for a spectacular stairway whose design came to Michelangelo in a dream. At a time when architects followed rules of strict proportions, Michelangelo created powerful curved steps that poured down from the reading room. He even designed the carved benches in the library.

Incredible Individuals

Andrea Palladio (1508–1580) is possibly the most important 16th century architect of northern Italy. His *palazzi* and villas, such as La Rotonda, and his *The Four Books of Architecture* influenced Western architects for centuries. It created a new style of architecture in later times called Palladianism in his honour.

▲ *Statue of Andrea Palladio in Vicenza, Italy*

▲ *The staircase in the Laurentian Library*

◀ *Laurentian Library (Biblioteca Medicea Laurenziana) is a historical library in Florence, Italy. It was built in the cloister of the Basilica of San Lorenzo under the patronage of Pope Clement VII*

Boboli Gardens

Located behind the fabulous Palazzo Pitti, the Boboli Gardens were created for the Medicis. Boboli is like a museum of multicoloured plants and amazing statues. The mixture of art and nature is characteristic of the Renaissance.

 ## The Architects

Boboli Gardens were originally designed by Niccolò Tribolo. After his death, Bartolomeo Ammannati (1511–1592) took over and later Bernardo Buontalenti (1531–1608). Many other people helped complete the gardens including Davide Fortini and Giorgio Vasari. However, they all followed the original design.

▲ *Powerful sculptures overlook the city of Florence*

▲ *Green alley in Boboli Gardens, Florence*

 ## The Amphitheatre

While designing the garden, Niccolò Tribolo thought to use the quarry at the base of the hill to build a great, horseshoe-shaped amphitheatre. This idea was brought to life after his death by several architects. In 1599, steps were added to it. Niches were built and filled with bronze statues and clay urns. Ancient Roman artefacts were added in later times. These include a granite basin from the Baths of Caracalla and an obelisk, which was brought from Egypt to Rome in 30 BCE, and from Rome to Boboli in 1790.

▶ *A view of the amphitheatre from Palazzo Pitti*

Palazzo Pitti

In the mid 15th century, Florentine banker Luca Pitti constructed a palazzo by the River Arno. It was perhaps designed by Luca Fancelli for a project by Filippo Brunelleschi. After Pitti's death, the Medicis took over the unfinished palace. Cosimo I and his wife Eleonora charged Bartolomeo Ammannati with the task of converting it into a princely palace. Ammannati doubled its volume, added side wings and created a most awe-inspiring Renaissance palace.

▲ *The garden-facing facade of Palazzo Pitti with the Roman granite basin and Egyptian obelisk at the centre*

Grottoes

Mannerist gardens usually feature artificial grottoes. The wonderful Buontalenti Grotto lies opposite the entrance to Boboli. It has three linked chambers with stucco decorations and frescoes showing mythological tales. Most famous are the rural scenes painted by Bernardino Poccetti (1548–1612). Sculptor Vincenzo de' Rossi (1525–1587) added statues of the Trojan prince Paris kidnapping Helen, queen of Sparta. The third chamber holds a basin with the goddess Venus sculpted by Giambologna.

▲ *Part of the Buontalenti Grotto showing stucco work, frescoes and the statues of Paris and Helen*

Amazing Statues

A number of Giambologna's most important sculptures are found at the Boboli Gardens. The amazing Fountain of the Ocean is one of these. At its granite centre stands Neptune. He is surrounded by river gods representing the Nile, Ganges and Euphrates. The statue stands at the Isolotto, an islet laid out by Alfonso Parigi in the middle of a pond. Another fantastic sculpture is the Dwarf Morgante, a fat, nude dwarf riding a tortoise. It symbolises laziness and wisdom.

▶ *Statue of Andromeda at the Isolotto; in the background is the Fountain of the Ocean*

Religious Architecture

Over the 15th and 16th centuries, architects such as Bramante, Palladio, Antonio da Sangallo the Younger, and Vincenzo Scamozzi showed a mastery over Classical styles. They revived these elements in churches and basilicas. Yet, they added their own personal inspiration to build never-before-seen structures. In the later days, their style became more ornamental. They incorporated statuary and decorative **cupolas**.

▲ *Donato Bramante*

▲ *Andrea Palladio*

▲ *Antonio da Sangallo the Younger*

▲ *Vincenzo Scamozzi*

Tempietto

In Rome, Bramante caught the eye of Cardinal Della Rovere, who later became Pope Julius II. For him, Bramante created one of the deeply harmonious *tempietto* (small chapel) of San Pietro in Montorio. The church was commissioned by Ferdinand and Isabella, rulers of Spain. It is believed that St. Peter was crucified at this very spot. Built in 1502, the *tempietto* is a Classical circular building surrounded by columns. Bramante's dome, raised on slender columns, completes the sculpture-like temple.

◀ *The tempietto of San Pietro in Montorio*

⊛ Incredible Individuals

Donato Bramante (1444–1514) brought Early Renaissance to Milan and High Renaissance to Rome. He was more-or-less the court architect to Ludovico Sforza, the ruler of Milan. In this deeply Gothic town, Bramante built many churches in the Classical style. His greatest work here is perhaps the Santa Maria delle Grazie. However, Bramante's grandest contribution to the Renaissance is undoubtedly St. Peter's Basilica in Rome.

▲ *A section of Santa Maria delle Grazie, Milan*

Il Redentore

Located on the island of Giudecca in Venice, the 16th century Chiesa del Santissimo Redentore (Church of the Most Holy Redeemer) is better known as Il Redentore. It was built to thank God for saving the city from a horrific outbreak of the plague. Designed by Andrea Palladio, the church sits beautifully on the waterfront. Its dazzling white facade stands under a large dome, which is topped by a statue of Christ the Redeemer. Inside the church is a series of interconnected spaces between the entrance and the high altar. Many important paintings decorate the building. This Renaissance masterpiece was only completed after Palladio's death. His foreman, Antonio da Ponte, faithfully followed the original designs.

▲ *Il Redentore on the island of Giudecca, Venice*

Basilica Palladiana

One of Palladio's important early works, the Palazzo delle Ragione was redesigned by Palladio with the use of loggias, and thus came to be known as Basilica Palladiana. This Gothic original was decorated with red and yellow diamonds of Verona marble. This can still be seen behind Palladio's work. Palladio added his hallmark **serliana openings** to its white marble exterior. The ground floor is built in the Doric order. The upper floor is an enormous hall with Ionic supports. This is where the town's Grand Council met. The entire building is topped by a copper-lined roof like an inverted ship's hull.

▲ *Basilica Palladiana with its serliana windows and peculiar roof*

Church of San Giorgio Maggiore

Designed in 1566 by Palladio, the Church of San Giorgio Maggiore was finished in 1610 by the talented Vincenzo Scamozzi (1548–1616). The church dominates the island of San Giorgio Maggiore. Palladio's facade is typically Mannerist with Classical elements. This makes it look like an imposing ancient Roman temple with giant columns and triangular tops. On a sunny day, the spacious interior is filled with light. A screen of pillars separates the high altar from the choir beyond.

▶ *Church of San Giorgio Maggiore*

The Spread of Renaissance

During the 16ᵗʰ century, France and Spain rose to power. Other European countries began to compete for power too. These included the Low Countries (modern-day Belgium, Luxembourg, and the Netherlands), England, Germany, and Russia. The Renaissance spirit was fully formed by this time. At the height of its glory, it found its way to various courts across Europe. However, in each country, the Classical style of architecture was adapted to suit local tastes and traditions. It is not always clear what buildings qualify as Renaissance. Many are more easily classified as Mannerist buildings. Indeed, it can be difficult to clearly see the start, the end, or the influence of Renaissance architecture in many European nations.

▲ Inigo Jones's arcaded central square at Covent Garden, London, was inspired by Renaissance piazzas (town squares) of Venice and Florence

▲ The City Hall at Delft is a Mannerist building. It was built in 1618–1620 by Hendrick de Keyser, who helped establish the Dutch Renaissance style

 ## Spain & Portugal

Spanish and Portuguese Renaissance follow similar paths. In Spain, this period can be divided into three phases. Its early Renaissance architecture is called Plateresque. This began in the late 15ᵗʰ century and lasted till about 1560. The period 1525–1560 showed a true adoption of Classical styles. The last phase, from 1560 to the end of the 16ᵗʰ century, is called Herreran. It is named after Juan de Herrera, the most important Spanish architect of the time. The buildings of this period are severe looking.

▲ The severe, grey domes of the San Lorenzo de El Escorial, Spain, is characteristic of the Herreran style of architecture

 ## Manueline Architecture

In Portugal, the architecture of the late 15ᵗʰ and early 16ᵗʰ centuries is called Manueline. It is named after the ruling king of the period, Manuel I. The style is very decorative and not truly Classical. Instead, it uses small Classical motifs as ornaments on Gothic-style buildings. The abundance of decorations reflects the wealth of maritime Portugal. Towards the end of the 16ᵗʰ century, architect Filippo Terzi created austere buildings in Portugal, such as the church of São Vicente de Fora in Lisbon. These were similar to Herrera's style.

▲ Belém Tower in Lisbon shows Renaissance motifs incorporated into the grand Manueline style

Convent of Christ, Tomar

After the mid 16th century, Portugal saw a truly Classical style. This can be seen in the work of the talented Diogo de Torralva at the cloister of the Convent of Christ (1557–1562). Located in the town of Tomar, its rhythmic bays show alternating arches and Classical columns. The mix of Doric and Ionic orders is similar to the Italian High Renaissance.

▲ The cloister of John III at the Convent of Christ, Tomar

In Real Life

The intelligent and cultured King Francis I invited Leonardo da Vinci to France. Da Vinci came with his artworks, many of which remained in the country. Even today, France has the largest collection of the master's paintings. This includes the famous *Mona Lisa*, known as *La Joconde* in France.

▶ *Statue of Leonardo da Vinci in Milan, Italy*

France

The French Renaissance is best seen in its 16th century *châteaus* (country mansions). The earliest influence of the period is seen in Loire Valley's Château d'Amboise. During the Renaissance, on the orders of Charles VII, Louis XII, and Francis I, the château was refurnished. Renaissance aesthetics blossomed under Francis I. It developed into French Mannerism, also called Henry II style.

▼ *The domed Château de Chantilly is representative of Henry II style, a type of Northern Mannerism that dominated France over the 16th century*

Renaissance Architecture in France

Over 1494–1525, France launched many invasions against Italy. Thats when French kings and aristocrats came under the spell of the Renaissance. For 25 years, during the reigns of Louis XII (1462–1515) and Francis I (1494–1547), the French owned the city of Milan. It was the capital city of Lombardy in northern Italy. It was then that the Lombard Renaissance style first appeared in France. Early French Renaissance was followed by a Mannerist period that dominated France till the end of the 16th century.

▲ *Château d'Azay-le-Rideau in the Loire Valley*

 ## Château de Chenonceau

Possibly the first French architect to gain a universal outlook on architecture like the Italians was Philibert de l'Orme (c. 1510–1570). He added a graceful Renaissance touch to the older, medieval Château de Chenonceau. He built a five-arched bridge to connect the château on the north bank of the river to the south bank.

▲ *The medieval Château d'Ussé with its Renaissance courtyard is said to have inspired the castle in Charles Perrault's fairy tale, Sleeping Beauty*

◀ *The Renaissance bridge of the Château de Chenonceau*

A Noble Style

Most middle-class families continued to patronise their home-grown Gothic style. It was the aristocracy that adopted the new Classical style. During the time of Louis XII and the early reign of Francis I, the French capital lay in Tours, near the Loire Valley. Thus, the towns in the valley were the earliest to express Classical architecture. This can be seen today in the châteaus of Amboise and Blois. In many cases, the new buildings, gardens, and courtyards were added to older medieval castles.

▲ At the Gothic Château de Blois, the wing of Francis I was built over 1515–1524 and shows greater influence of Classical Italian styles

Château de Chambord

The largest early French Renaissance building is the hunting lodge built from 1519 for Francis I at Chambord. The vast château is 156 metres long with a rectangular court. The surrounding wall has round towers at the corners. The genius of Leonardo da Vinci can be seen, in the central staircase and the inventive ventilation system of the château. He had been invited to France by Francis I, who admired him. To cap it all, the château is fortified and protected by a moat. It is set in a garden surrounded by a 32-km-long wall.

▶ Frenchman Pierre Lescot (c. 1515–1578) established the grand Mannerist French Renaissance style, best seen in the rebuilding of the Louvre Palace that he did for Francis I

◀ Château de Chambord

Dutch and Flemish Renaissance

The area occupied by modern-day Belgium, Luxembourg, and the Netherlands is historically called the Low Countries. The Flemish and Dutch people of this region had Gothic preferences until the 17th century. At most, Classical motifs—similar to those in France—were added on as decorations to Gothic buildings. These can be seen in some 16th century buildings in Flanders (northern Belgium), which had strong trade relations with the rest of Europe. In the early 17th century, Dutch sculptor and architect Hendrick de Keyser developed the Renaissance style in the Netherlands. His wonderful Mannerist creations were so unique that he was made the municipal architect of Amsterdam. Another important figure was Hans Vredeman de Vries who became famous as a garden architect.

▲ Designed by Gothic architect Rombout Keldermans, the Palace of Margaret of Austria showcases formal Renaissance motifs

Architects

Some of the earliest and most notable architects who took inspiration from Classicism were Lieven de Key (1560–1627), Hendrick de Keyser (1565–1621), and Cornelis Danckerts de Ry (1561–1634). Lieven de Key is most famous for building Haarlem's Meat Market. As the 17th century progressed, people began to look for purer Renaissance forms. Among the architects who developed the new style were the celebrated Jacob van Campen (1596–1657), Philips Vingboons (1607–1678), and Pieter Post (1608–1669). The gigantic Town Hall of Amsterdam constructed over 1648–1655, is one of van Campen's masterworks. It was converted into the royal palace in 1806 when Napoleon Bonaparte set his brother upon the Dutch throne.

▲ The Town Hall of Amsterdam features sculptures in the style of Dutch Classicism symbolising justice and commerce

▲ Originally built around 1633–1644 as a residence for Count Johan Maurits van Nassau-Siegen, the Mauritshuis was designed by Jacob van Campen and built by Pieter Post in the Dutch Classical style

In Real Life

Built over 1602–1603 by Lieven de Key using costly materials, the beautiful Vleeshal (literally, meat hall) was the only place in Haarlem allowed to sell fresh meat until 19th century!

🏛 Stadhuis

The most eye-catching building of the Flemish Renaissance is the Stadhuis (Town Hall) of Antwerp. It was designed by Flemish architect Loys du Foys, and Italian architect Nicolo Scarini and executed by Cornelis Floris II over 1561–1565. The building replaced Antwerp's smaller medieval town hall to show the city's prosperity as a trade port. The town hall follows the stern repeating symmetry common in Classical architecture. It is softened by a wealth of detail unique to the Low Countries. Doric and Ionic **pilasters** separate the large windows.

▲ The Town Hall at Antwerp

💡 Isn't It Amazing!

Classical caryatids are stone carvings of draped women. Hans Vredeman de Vries's imaginative caryatids from c. 1565 show how such Classical motifs changed in the Low Countries.

▲ Hans Vredeman de Vries's angular caryatids from his architectural drawings

🏛 Grand Place

Guilds are formed when professionals for instance, artists or merchants, come together in groups to oversee practice and fair play in their trade. In the Low Countries, many guilds from the 15th and 16th centuries were wealthy and powerful. They built guild houses and private homes that reflected the incoming architectural styles from Italy—or what they understood of it. The grand town square of the bustling city of Brussels is surrounded by such buildings. Unlike the stern Classical Italian buildings though, the houses around the Grand Place are gaudy/ fancy and opulent. They are ornamented with extravagant statues and motifs that include phoenixes, horses, scrolls, urns, fluted pillars, and lace-like details.

▲ Grand Place (central square) is adorned every other year with thousands of begonias for the Brussels Flower Carpet event

▲ Roman statuary and roundels adorning the showy facade of La Louve, the house of the guild of archers, at Grand Place

The Iberian Peninsula

The southwest corner of Europe is a large peninsula called Iberia. It is mostly taken up by the countries of Spain and Portugal. During the Middle Ages, it was inhabited by Islamic citizens of Arab, Spanish, and North African origins. The Catholic kingdoms called them the Moors and drove them out of Spain by 1492. However, the newly Catholic peninsula admired the Moorish architecture left behind. When the Italian Renaissance entered Spain and Portugal, it could not completely dislodge this inheritance.

▲ *The Alcázar of Toledo, was originally a Roman palace. Its facade and courtyard were rebuilt in the Renaissance style by Spanish architect Alonso de Covarrubias (1488–1570)*

 ## Plateresque Spain

From the Catholic occupation of Spain in 1492 till about 1560, Spanish architecture went through a phase called Plateresque. There was no real change in the proportions or designs of buildings. Instead, Italian artisans who came over to create tombs or altars introduced Renaissance terms to the Spaniards. Spanish architects experimented with decorative pilasters and arabesques. However, the splendour-loving culture of Spain was markedly different from the stern Classicism of Renaissance Italy. Thus, the changes were purely ornamental.

▲ *The Royal Hospital at Santiago de Compostela was built over 1501–1511 by Enrique de Egas. Its ornamented facade is interspersed with large expanses of bare wall*

 ## The Town Hall of Seville

The construction for the outstanding Ayuntamiento (Town Hall) of Seville was started in 1527 by Diego de Riaño. The building shows the influence of Lombard Renaissance in its panelled pilasters and relief-covered half-columns. Numerous medallions lie on the walls, under the windows, and between the pilasters.

◀ *The Plateresque facade of Seville's Town Hall*

Renaissance Portugal

The reign of Manuel I (1469–1521) was a time of great wealth for Portugal. As most of these riches came from sea trade, Manueline decorations were naturally ocean-themed. Coral motifs, barnacle-encrusted mouldings and carvings of seaweed and algae were popular. Anchors, stone ropes and seafaring instruments were seen over windows and doors. This unique style existed between the Gothic and Renaissance phases in Portugal.

Classical Period

The Classical style first appeared in Portugal in 1526 in the Palace of Charles V within the complex of the amazing Alhambra, the magnificent Moorish palace-fortress. It was designed by Pedro Machuca, a Spaniard who had studied in Italy. As Holy Roman Emperor, Charles V dominated European politics. His palace was to be a statement of his power. However, the palace was never really completed. It is a square building with a circular courtyard that is 30 m in diameter. The arena is surrounded by a colonnade with austere Doric and Ionic columns. The plan is thus, truly Classical with the correct harmony of proportions.

▲ A window at the Convent of Christ in Tomar showcases Manueline decorations

▲ The central courtyard of the Palace of Charles V was intended for bullfights and tournaments

Herreran Architecture

The culmination of Spanish Renaissance occurred with the Herreran style. It is named after Juan de Herrera (c. 1530–1597), the architect of Imperial Spain in the 16th century. The finest example of his work is the El Escorial palace built for Philip II, the son of Charles V. While the father brought Renaissance to Spain, the son promoted more Mannerist creations. Herreran architecture enforced geometrical principals and clean spaces. Decorations were kept to a minimum.

☀ Isn't It Amazing!

Some of the best examples of Plateresque style can be seen in the historic town of Salamanca. The Monterrey Palace, built in 1539 by Rodrigo Gil de Hontañon and Martín de Santiago, even inspired architects of the 19th and early 20th centuries! The Convento de las Dueñas and the Casa de las Muertes (House of the Dead) are two other Plateresque gems.

▲ Hans Vredeman de Vries's angular caryatids from his architectural drawings

◄ The Collegiate Church of San Pedro, Lerma, exemplifies the clean-cut facade of the Herreran style

El Escorial

The Royal Monastery of San Lorenzo de El Escorial was built by King Philip II of Spain. The complex holds a royal palace and a vast monastery. Rising from the foothills of the Sierra de Guadarrama mountains, the complex is a massive rectangle measuring 206x161 metres. The devout Philip II established a basilica at its centre. This is one of the few religious structures outside Italy to use the Classical style of architecture. Construction began in 1563 under the Spanish Renaissance architect Juan Bautista de Toledo. He is thought to be responsible for the plans, style, and execution of El Escorial. After his death in 1567, his assistant Juan de Herrera took over and made many alterations.

Philip's Necropolis

El Escorial was constructed on the site of an older monastery. Philip II wanted a place where all the Spanish rulers could be buried. He thus, actively took part in the planning of the complex. In particular, the king removed anything that seemed decorative or showy. El Escorial is thus, a massive, forbidding structure with plain walls, and seemingly endless rows of windows. The austere facade is constructed entirely of grey granite. The interior is equally severe and lack in decoration. A few Classical touches are seen in the use of Doric columns and plain arches.

▲ The Courtyard of the Kings and an entrance to the basilica

▼ The vast and serene monastery at El Escorial

Incredible Individuals

During the 1557 Battle of Saint Quentin, the Spanish army is said to have destroyed a church dedicated to St Lawrence. Philip II supposedly dedicated the monastery at El Escorial to St. Lawrence to atone for the destruction.

The Layout

Juan de Toledo's ambitious design for this part-royal court, part-monastic construction took form in over a year. His ground plan is thought to represent the grid of hot coals on which Saint Lawrence was martyred. The

▲ *Western facade showing the main entrance to the basilica and the monastery's front yard*

royal gardens lie to the east and the monastery gardens to the south. The outer buildings form a perfect square and are four stories high with square towers at the corners. They enclose the inner complex like a fortress. Beyond the central church runs the monastery's **cloister**, which encloses the Courtyard of the Evangelists, one of Herrera's fine creations.

The Church

The Courtyard of the Kings opens beyond the main entrance. It is dominated by the central structure, which is the basilica. This serene building is topped by a massive cupola that was inspired by Michelangelo's dome for St Peter's Basilica in Rome. Two striking bell towers rise cleanly on either side.

▶ *The high altar inside the basilica is supported by Ionic columns*

Isn't It Amazing!

Philip II founded the library at El Escorial. The room, with its marble floors, beautiful wooden shelves, and amazing painted ceiling, is home to more than 4,700 rare manuscripts—including **illuminated manuscripts**. There are also some 40,000 printed books in the collection.

▲ *The El Escorial library*

The Monastery

Toledo's monastery was a great rectangle made of three parts. On the south were five cloisters, which included the palace and offices. The monks' living quarters lay in the north.

▶ *El Escorial, home of the kings of Spain*

The British Isles

During the 15th and 16th centuries, England was largely on bad terms with the Pope and the Holy Roman Emperor. First, Henry VIII of England broke away from the Catholic Church and set himself up as the head of the Protestant English Church. Later, his daughter Queen Elizabeth I went to war with Philip II of Spain, a devout and powerful Catholic monarch. As a result, there is little true Renaissance architecture in England. Instead, the evolving styles of this period are named after the rulers—Tudor style (after the house of Henry VIII), Elizabethan style, and Jacobean style (after James I of England).

▲ *Hatfield House is a grand Jacobean country house set in formal gardens*

 ## Identifying the Styles

The Tudor style used Renaissance decorations on native Gothic designs. Such adornments included low arches, rows of rectangular windows, and patterned brickwork. This is mostly seen in secular buildings such as the Hampton Court Palace. In Elizabethan times, the houses changed into tall, rectangular buildings. Windows became mullioned and used a great deal of glass. The Jacobean age saw the style becoming more consistent and formal. The buildings included Classical columns and arched galleries, though still adorned with fanciful details. Throughout the Renaissance period, English courtiers built prodigy houses. These were showy country mansions meant to attract visits from the reigning king and queen.

 ## Incredible Individuals

Towards the end of Queen Elizabeth's rule, the painter and architect Inigo Jones (1573–1652) brought real Renaissance designs to England. His bold work with Classical proportions and detail was inspired by the theories of Andrea Palladio. The Banqueting House at Whitehall is one of his few remaining masterworks.

▶ *Inigo Jones*

▲ *Decorative Tudor brickwork on the chimneys of Hampton Court*

▶ *Bess of Hardwick, the richest women after the Queen herself during Elizabethan times, built her house with such massive windows that it led to the popular rhyme, 'Hardwick Hall, more glass than wall'. Glass was indeed a luxury during this period*

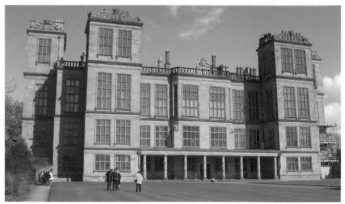

Hampton Court

The unintentional symmetry of Hampton Court makes it appear more Classical than Gothic. The palace was constructed by Cardinal Wolsey in 1515 and later taken over by Henry VIII. Its Renaissance elements are largely decorative. For instance, a number of terracotta roundels by the Italian sculptor Giovanni da Maiano adorn the gateways.

Longleat

Built by the statesman Sir John Thynne (1515–1580), Longleat is one of Elizabethan England's finest **prodigy houses**. It was constructed with the help of Robert Smythson, a leading architect of the time, and a number of other designers. The building was arranged symmetrically around two courts. The third story was most likely added after Thynne's death. The three stories follow the Classic orders of Doric, Ionic and Corinthian style.

▲ *Bust of Roman Emperor Tiberius decorating Hampton Court*

▲ *Longleat House*

Wollaton Hall

One of Robert Smythson's most amazing buildings, the symmetrical Wollaton Hall is basically square with square towers at four corners. The great hall lies at the centre and rises above the rest of the building. Despite this basic plan, the house looks sensational with its mullioned windows, arched niches, columns and many Classical touches. The playful exaggerations are similar to Italian Mannerism. The corner towers are decorated with Flemish strapwork, which are raised and curved bands that look like leather straps.

▲ *Wollaton Hall*

RENAISSANCE ART

RENAISSANCE ART

The period between 1400–1600 saw a revival of Greek and Roman art styles in Europe. This period is therefore called **Renaissance**, the French word for 'rebirth'. Artists adopted oil paintings and created sculptures in marble and bronze. Attention to light, detail, and colour were hallmarks of the Renaissance in northern Europe.

Some of the greatest contributions to Renaissance art came from the Italian states of Florence, Rome, and Venice. It was driven by the ideas of **humanism**, which reject religious stereotypes and focus on the individual. Artists studied human bodies to understand movement and expression. Many new techniques were developed to express reality in art.

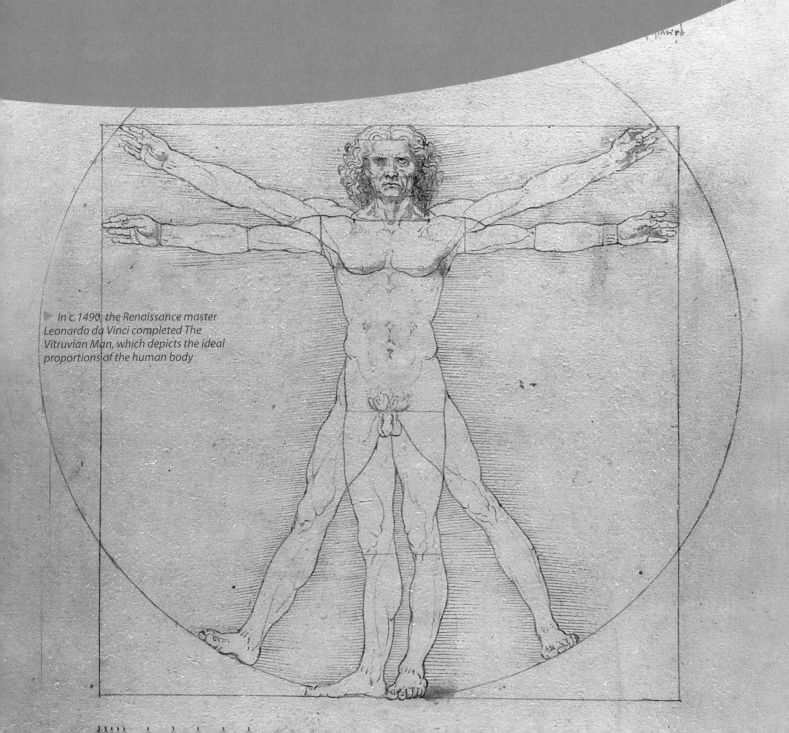

▶ In c. 1490, the Renaissance master Leonardo da Vinci completed The Vitruvian Man, which depicts the ideal proportions of the human body

Renaissance in the Low Countries

'Low Countries' is the historic name for the area covering the present-day countries of **Belgium, Luxembourg, and the Netherlands.** The people who lived here were Dutch and Flemish. Their Renaissance extended over the 15th and 16th centuries. In the early years, most artworks were made for the Church. Around 1530, the region split along religious lines, into Flemish Catholics and Dutch Protestants. This divide is also reflected in the art from the Renaissance period.

 ## Van Eyck Brothers

The Flemish brothers Hubert van Eyck (c.1366–1426) and Jan van Eyck (c.1390–1441) were the founders and masters of the Netherlandish Renaissance. Working with oil paints, they reached a level of brilliance never seen before. The Ghent Altarpiece at St. Bavo's Cathedral is their masterpiece. The side panels of this **polyptych** could be folded over the central panels. It shows Christ the King, Virgin Mary and John the Baptist looking upon a gathering of saints, sinners, priests and soldiers. They attend the adoration of Jesus, who appears as the Lamb of God. At the very end are Adam and Eve.

▲ The open view of the Ghent Altarpiece, done with oil paints on wooden panels, c.1432

▲ The closed view of the Ghent Altarpiece shows prophets, patrons and angels

 ## The Arnolfini Portrait

Jan van Eyck left behind many works. One of his most famous works is the *Arnolfini Portrait* (1434), which shows a wealthy businessman and his expectant wife. In an era when most art was religious and public, this unusual piece was secular and private.

Van Eyck used layer after layer of paint to give a bright, mirror-like effect to the whole picture. Oil paint allowed him to create fine details. Notice the vivid textures of wood, velvet, metal, etc., the careful folds of the clothes and the many variations of light. The portrait looks as real as life—a breakthrough effect of the Renaissance.

▶ The portrait was supposedly of Giovanni Arnolfini and his wife

Robert Campin and Rogier van der Weyden

The van Eyck brothers painted for the nobility. On the other hand, Robert Campin (c.1378–1444) painted for middle-class patrons. He is also called the Master of Flémalle for his Flemish style of painting. His most famous pupil is Rogier van der Weyden. The works of both artists show deep emotions and religious passion. Van der Weyden is particularly known for creating interesting spaces and slender figures.

▲ Campin's, *The Merode Altarpiece was a triptych (3-panel art) of the Annunciation, showing how the stiff and flat styles of Gothic art were turning into the more realistic forms of Renaissance art*

▲ *Van der Weyden's, The Descent from the Cross, painted in primary colours, shows incredibly realistic emotion and movement*

Hieronymus Bosch

In the 15th century, the Netherlands was full of religious fanatics. Their extreme behaviour inspired Bosch's paintings. He painted Heaven, Hell, and Earth, using fabulous landscapes and dream-like images. Bosch's **surreal** art is filled with **symbolism**.

▶ *The Garden of Earthly Delights shows the Garden of Eden and Hell on the left and right respectively. In between lies a busy world of human activity. Each group of figures tells its own story*

Pieter Bruegel the Elder

Flemish master Pieter Bruegel the Elder (c.1525–1569) painted amazing and large compositions. Mountains, rivers, cities, and ships were a part of his landscapes. Each work had a moral lesson. His *Tower of Babel* is a warning against arrogance. The works also show great attention to detail and a sensitive use of light and shade.

◀ *The Tower of Babel, 1563*

German Renaissance

Renaissance took off in the modern regions of Germany and Austria around 1450. It was aided by the invention of the printing press by the German inventor, Johannes Gutenberg. There were also other innovations, such as oil-based ink and many types of moulds and matrices, that spread the ideas of Renaissance. As a result, printmaking, woodcuts, etchings, and engravings dominated the German Renaissance. Religious panel paintings and wood carvings were also popular.

▲ The carved and painted centrepiece of the St Wolfgang Altarpiece is a masterwork of sculptor-painter Michael Pacher, one of the earliest artists to introduce Renaissance principles to Germany

▲ Court painter Lucas Cranach the Elder (1472–1553) drew many portraits, including one of his friend Martin Luther, the man who brought about Protestantism, a new form of Christianity

▲ The printmaker Martin Schongauer is famous for his Madonna of the Rose Garden (1473)

Albrecht Dürer (1471–1528)

Albrecht Dürer is possibly the greatest figure of the German Renaissance. He was the son of a goldsmith. Inspired by the High Renaissance of Italy, Dürer learned mathematics and geometry to perfect his art. These helped him create harmony and realism in his compositions. Dürer also studied **anatomy** and human nature. As a result, his line drawings seemed to have a life of their own. Dürer's talent also lay in using magnificent colours and a particular way of painting light.

▲ Dürer's skill as a draughtsman can be seen in a 1508 piece called *Praying Hands*

◄ One of Dürer's most famous paintings depicts the martyrdom of 10,000 Christian soldiers on Mount Ararat, carried out by Shahpur I, the King of Persia, under orders from the Roman Emperor

▲ Albrecht Dürer's self-portrait at the age of 28

Matthias Grünewald (c.1470–1528)

Little is known about Matthias Grünewald, a skilled Renaissance creator of Christian art in Germany. His colouring techniques were centuries ahead of his time. Because of this, only a few contemporaries understood his genius. His greatest work perhaps was displayed in the hospital of the Monastery of St Anthony in Isenheim. It is called the Isenheim Altarpiece and is a polyptych. When closed, it shows the crucifixion of Christ. Christ's agony is shown in his painfully thin and marred body with horrific large nails driven through his hands and feet. This realistic and symbolic torment of the saviour is meant to reflect pain of the patients and their families who were all too familiar with; but there is also the hope of salvation.

◀ *The Isenheim Altarpiece created between 1512 and 1516*

Hans Holbein the Younger (1497–1543)

While Gothic art is focused on the divine, Renaissance is all about the human condition. Influenced by Humanism, the brilliant Hans Holbein became the greatest portrait painter of Europe during his lifetime. Before he had turned 20, he was already famous for his portraits of *Erasmus of Rotterdam* (1523), the *Darmstadt Madonna* (1526), the *Astronomer Nicholas Kratzer* (1528), and *Sir Thomas More* (1527).

In 1532, Holbein became the artist of the English court. With skill and precision, he made magnificent portraits of King Henry VIII, Thomas Cromwell and many others. He also created festive paintings and designs for jewellery and precious objects.

▲ *Holbein's painting of the English lawyer and statesman, Sir Thomas More, who was executed by Henry VIII for upholding his religious beliefs*

The Cologne School of Art

During the Renaissance, Cologne was a wealthy and secure city. Most important among the painters from the Cologne School of

Art was the precise, detailed artist Stefan Lochner (c.1410–1451). He created a soft style of oil painting noted for its amazing hues and delicate emotions.

◀ *Lochner's altarpieces used flowing lines and gem-like colours, as seen in this painting called the Last Judgement (c.1435)*

💡 Isn't It Amazing!

Holbein produced over 1,200 drawings from woodcuts! The best-known series amongst these is called the *Dance of Death*. It shows a skeletal death mocking humanity, from emperors and judges, to merchants and farmers.

Quattrocento

In Italy, the artistic period of the 15th century is called the Quattrocento. Italy was not a unified country but a group of independent city-states. Among them were Florence, Rome, and Venice. The Renaissance flourished foremost in these three cities.

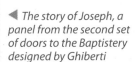
▶ *Art of the Quattrocento moved away from divine perfection to the study of the individual. This is captured in the sinuous bodies and brutal emotions of Hercules and Antaeus, a bronze statue by Antonio del Pollaiuolo*

 ## From the Beginning

The Quattrocento began in Florence with a competition over who would design the eastern doors of the **Baptistery** of San Giovanni. It was won by the goldsmith and painter Lorenzo Ghiberti. Filippo Brunelleschi, and Donatello, who were defeated in the competition, left for Rome. There, they studied the sculpture and architecture of ancient Rome. When they returned to Florence, they put their Classical knowledge to practical use. Thus began the Renaissance.

◀ *The major Italian city-states of the late 15ᵗʰ century*

◀ *The story of Joseph, a panel from the second set of doors to the Baptistery designed by Ghiberti*

 ## A Matter of Perspective

Have you ever noticed that faraway objects look smaller than the objects that are close by? A tree outside your window will look smaller than the pencil in your hand. This is because the brain does not see things as they are. It sees objects relative to the position of other objects. This manner of seeing things is called perspective.

Naturally, your perspective changes when you move. Drawing sizes, angles, and shapes of objects drawn according to perspective needs a lot of practice and skill. It also needs an understanding of maths and geometry. Such mathematical knowledge was brought back into art by Renaissance sculptor and designer Filippo Brunelleschi. It spread across Europe and other artists too added their own knowledge to it. It is seen as a hallmark of Renaissance art.

▶ *Andrea Mantegna (1431–1506) painted St. Sebastian to look like a sculpture. He also played with perspective by lowering the horizon. This gives the whole piece a monumental appearance*

Donatello (1386–1466)

Donato di Niccolò di Betto Bardi is better known simply as Donatello. He is often thought to be the finest sculptor of the Quattrocento. He put such movement and emotion into his statues that they seemed to come alive. Donatello's masterpiece is a 5-foot-tall, bronze sculpture of David. The young Biblical shepherd is seen as a slender, confident boy wearing a hat and boots. He stands over the head of his enemy Goliath, who he has slain, holding Goliath's long sword.

▶ *An early bronze relief sculpture of Donatello, The Feast of Herod*

Andrea del Verrocchio (c.1435–1488)

Inspired by Donatello, Verrocchio created sculptures that were just as amazing. In particular, his statue of the **condottiere** Bartolomeo Colleoni (1480s) shows bold, swaggering movement. His bronze figure of a *putto* (a small boy, a cherub, or cupid) with a dolphin was a breakthrough in freestanding Renaissance sculpture. The boy is balanced on one leg and looks like he could topple over, but he does not. In fact, the overall design gives every angle of this figure equal importance.

Lady with Primroses

Created over 1475–1480, the *Lady with Primroses* created a new type of Renaissance **bust**. As with ancient Roman statues, the arms were also shown here. This allowed the artist to express emotion through the face as well as body language.

▶ *Verrocchio's Lady with Primroses shows a woman dreamily holding flowers to her bosom*

◀ *Putto with Dolphin, c.1470*

⊚ Incredible Individuals

Verrocchio was a talented painter. He owned a large studio-cum-workshop that attracted many, many students. Among them was none other than the foremost of Renaissance masters Leonardo da Vinci.

▶ *Experts believe that some parts of Verrocchio's painting Tobias and the Angel were done by Leonardo da Vinci*

Early Renaissance Paintings

The Italian Renaissance crept in during the 14ᵗʰ century, a time period called the Trecento. An early master painter of the period was Giotto di Bondone (c.1267–1337). He moved away from the flat and idealised drawings of the Gothic era. Instead, he made simple, clear paintings that were true to nature and showed the depths of humanity. For almost 700 years, he was worshipped as the Father of European painting. Tragically, 14ᵗʰ century Italy was devastated by terrible wars and the Great Plague. It was only in the *Quattrocento* that Renaissance painting truly took hold in Italy.

▲ *The Entry into Jerusalem by Giotto shows the gradual change from flat Gothic paintings to the emotional, individualistic figures of Renaissance*

▲ *The Queen of Sheba Meets King Solomon is part of The Legend of the True Cross, a series of early Renaissance frescoes by Piero della Francesca, an artist and mathematician*

Masaccio (1401–1428)

The founder and the first master of *Quattrocento* paintings is nicknamed Masaccio. The first 21 years of his life are not documented. But, in just six years, he entirely changed the style of Florentine painting. Though he lived a short life, his work laid the foundations for Western art. Masaccio's work showed scholarly thinking. It was composed on a grand scale. He introduced a never-before-seen degree of Naturalism into each painting.

◀ *Masaccio's Holy Trinity is painted in such a way, it appears to be three-dimensional. This technique is called the tromp l'oeil, meaning deceiving the eye*

The Brancacci Chapel

Over 1425–1427, Masaccio painted a series of frescoes inspired by the life of St Peter. Located in the Brancacci Chapel, these masterpieces are large and dramatic. The painting of Adam and Eve, as they are expelled from the Garden of Eden, shows the couple writhing in distress. Eve's expression especially shows a feeling of great despair. After Masaccio's death, the Renaissance talent Filippino Lippi completed the fresco cycle.

▶ *Masaccio's Expulsion of Adam and Eve, 1427*

▲ *St. Peter heals a disabled person and raises Tabitha from the dead, a Brancacci fresco by Masaccio*

 # Fra Angelico (1400–1455)

Guido di Pietro, also called Fra Angelico, is one of the greatest 15th century painters. His early Renaissance work reflects a calm and religious style. Strongly influenced by Classical Rome, Fra Angelico carefully composed his paintings according to the rules of perspective.

Fra Filippo Lippi (1406–1469)

Though deeply influenced by Masaccio and Angelico, Fra Filippo Lippi had his own style of painting. His *Coronation of the Virgin* is a historic and complex piece. It is the first example of a single vast scene spread over multiple panels. The painter Fra Diamante was Lippi's companion and colleague. Together, they decorated parts of the cathedral of Prato, a lively city near Florence. His work at the cathedral is some of Lippi's best art.

▶ *Adoration in the Forest by Fra Filippo Lippi, 1459*

Sandro Botticelli (1445–1510)

Fra Lippi's most famous student, Botticelli, created paintings filled with the spirit of Renaissance. His world-famous *Birth of Venus* and *Primavera* showcase his love for pale colours and graceful figures. Botticelli painted fanciful, yet deeply symbolic scenes from mythology.

◀ *Commissioned by the Pope, Angelico's St Lawrence Distributing Alms (1447) uses lavish designs, expensive colours, gilded figures, and gold leaf motifs*

▲ *Primavera (Spring) by Botticelli shows mythological figures in a garden*

◀ *The Birth of Venus shows the Roman Goddess of love risen from the sea. To her left are the wind god Zephyr and the nymph Chloris or Aura. To her right is an attendant goddess bearing a cloak*

The Medici Influence

The Medicis were a wealthy merchant family of Florence. They rose to fame in the 15th century after Giovanni de Medici set up a successful bank. At the time, Florence was recovering from a dreadful plague and economic disasters. Medici money revived the city. Giovanni's son Cosimo became the primary figure in Florence in 1434. For most of the next 200 years, the Medicis ruled the city-state. They even married into royalty. Both Catherine de' Medici (1519–1589) and Marie de' Medici (1573–1642) were queens of France. Four of the Medicis became Popes. They were Leo X (1475–1521), Clement VII (1478–1534), Pius IV (1499–1565), and Leo XI (1535–1605).

▲ Leading members of the Medici court, created in the workshop of Mannerist artist Agnolo Bronzino (1503–1572)

▶ Paintings of Pope Clement VII during different stages of his life, by High Renaissance artist Sebastiano del Piombo (1485–1547)

▲ The Coronation of Marie de' Medici by the Baroque-period (17th century) genius, Peter Paul Rubens

Godfathers of the Renaissance

The Medicis were famous supporters of art and architecture. Their wealth allowed them to commission books, churches, sculptures, frescoes, paintings and all manner of valuable and beautiful objects. As a result of their interest, Florence attracted intelligent and talented men from everywhere. Among them were such talents as Brunelleschi, Masaccio, Donatello, Ghirlandaio, his pupil Michelangelo, Raphael, and many, many others. The Medicis also traded with major cities of Europe. Thus, they were able to acquire books and artworks from other parts of the world. The stability and generosity of the Medicis led to the Renaissance in Florence.

◀ Ghirlandaio's unique Confirmation of the Franciscan Rule depicts the Pope blessing St. Francis. In the foreground, the Medici sons climb up the stairs with their tutor. Waiting to receive them is a dark-haired Lorenzo de' Medici, also known as Lorenzo the Magnificent

👤 In Real Life

The Medicis not only patronised art and architecture, but also supported science. They funded the famous scientist Galileo Galilei, the father of modern astronomy. Galileo also taught the Medici family. When he first discovered the moons of Jupiter, he named them after the Medici sons. This was changed by later astronomers to honour Galileo himself.

▶ Galileo Galilei, by the Venetian portrait painter Domenico Tintoretto

Cosimo de' Medici (1389–1464)

It was under Cosimo de' Medici, the Elder, that Renaissance Florence began to take shape. Under his orders, numerous churches were built. Among them is San Marco, whose walls bear frescoes by Fra Angelico. Cosimo also commissioned the opulent Medici Palace, built by architect Michelozzo, a follower of Brunelleschi. It was decorated with magnificent paintings. Notably, a chapel inside contains Benozzo Gozzoli's fantastic *Procession of the Magi* stretching over three walls. Cosimo not only assured the artists of sufficient work, but also treated them as friends instead of labourers. Upon his death, the people of Florence named him *Pater Patriae* (Father of the Country).

▲ *The Procession of the Magi on the east wall; the golden-haired boy on the white horse represents the youngest Magi. He is drawn in the likeness of young Lorenzo de' Medici, who grew up to be Lorenzo the Magnificent. Behind him, at the head of the procession are two old men in red caps. These are Cosimo and his younger brother Piero Medici*

▲ *Detail of the youngest Magi*

▲ *Detail of Cosimo and Piero*

 ## Il Magnifico (1449–1492)

Lorenzo de' Medici was the principal citizen of Florence through the peak of Florence's Renaissance. He was nicknamed Il Magnifico (The Magnificent). He was as lavish as Cosimo in acquiring great works of art. Lorenzo himself was a talented poet. Artists under his patronage included Botticelli, Perugino, Ghirlandaio, Verrocchio, and Verrocchio's pupil, Leonardo da Vinci. It was in Lorenzo's sculpture garden that a young Michelangelo learned the Classical Arts.

◀ *Botticelli's Adoration of the Magi shows several members of the Medici family. Lorenzo or Giuliano stands with his sword to the far left; Cosimo is seen kneeling before the infant Christ*

Pope Leo X (1475–1521)

◀ *In 1518, Raphael painted a realistic portrait of Pope Leo X as a middle-aged man whose face reflects the turmoil (unrest) of his rule. He is shown with the cardinals Giulio de' Medici and Luigi de' Rossi*

Lorenzo's son and the first Medici pope, Leo X drew artists away from Florence to Rome and the Vatican. He borrowed and spent a lot of money to support the arts and even to fund a war. Leo X is often called the last of the High Renaissance popes. The artist Raphael greatly benefited from his efforts and created many iconic works of art.

▲ *Ceramic artist Nicola da Urbino created this large dish showing Pope Leo X presenting a baton to Federigo II Gonzaga*

Italian High Renaissance

The Quattrocento unofficially ended in 1503 when Cardinal Giuliano della Rovere became Pope Julius II. The Renaissance of 16th century Italy is called Cinquecento. Its first three decades saw the flowering of Renaissance art. This period is called High Renaissance. While the Medicis in Florence fostered Early Renaissance, the Popes paid for High Renaissance, centred in Rome. Separate schools of talent developed in Venice. The ideals of Classical and Humanistic art dominated painting and sculpture. Various techniques of perspective, shading, etc., were mastered to enhance Realism. The period began to decline after the Sack of Rome in 1527, when artists were forced to flee the city.

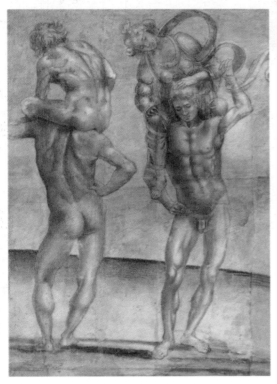

▲ *Artist Luca Signorelli's sketches show his attentiveness to human detail*

▶ *Raphael's Mass at Bolsena depicts a 13th century miracle. As seen in the zoomed-in panels, the artist painted himself, Pope Julius II, and the Pope's daughter Felice della Rovere into the fresco*

 ## Leading Lights

High Renaissance in Rome was led by three geniuses. Leonardo da Vinci, the master of oil painting and **sfumato**; Michelangelo, the greatest sculptor and fresco artist of his time; and Raphael, the finest painter of the period. Also noteworthy were Fra Bartolommeo and Andrea del Sarto (1486–1530). Outside Rome, the extraordinary Correggio (1494–1534) was the leading painter of the Parma school. His *Assumption of the Virgin*, painted onto the dome of Parma Cathedral, contained three-dimensional illusions of heaven. The frescoes of Luca Signorelli (c.1445–1523) can be seen in the Sistine Chapel and Orvieto Cathedral. They are said to have influenced Michelangelo's own masterpieces.

▶ *Fra Bartolommeo's Pietà shows dramatic depths and was inspired by the masterpieces of Michelangelo and Raphael*

▲ Correggio's Assumption of the Virgin (1526–1530) seems to spiral upward into the sky. It marks the path of the Virgin to Christ, who is seen waiting for her in heaven. The superb fresco had a deep impact on later artists

▶ Portrait of a Young Man, by Andrea del Sarto who was called an artist senza errori (without errors)

In Real Life

Leonardo da Vinci studied many subjects during his life including anatomy, flight, nature, mechanics, and so forth. His interests were so varied, he was constantly moving from one thing to another. As a result, he had little time to paint. His fame rests on just a handful of completed masterpieces.

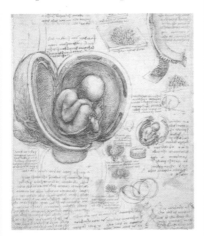

▲ A page from da Vinci's journal shows a baby growing in its mother's womb, a part of his research into human life

High Renaissance Aesthetics

Oil painting became immensely popular during the Renaissance. It allowed artists to add layers of colours, varying tones, and details till the perfection was achieved. Realism was still the main goal. Yet, High Renaissance art began to pay more attention to beauty and harmony. Nature was not simply copied as it is. Instead, it was depicted in its most dramatic or graceful moment. Like the ancient Greeks and Romans, Renaissance artists were looking for truth in natural forms. This led them to create ideals of perfection.

▶ The Tempest, one of the earliest realistic landscapes, was the work of Giorgione, a High Renaissance talent of Venice

The Perfect Human

The idealism of High Renaissance led artists to look for the 'ideal' human—one with harmonious build, muscular grace, oval face, triangular forehead, and a straight nose. Such a figure can be seen in Raphael's paintings and Michelangelo's sculptures. This manner of thinking, which attached more importance to human beings than to God, is called Humanism. It is expressed even in the religious works of High Renaissance artists. Such paintings would glorify Man, not God. However, there were still some mythological works that glorified God instead of Man. This is best seen in Correggio's *Jupiter and Io*, where the Roman god Jupiter meets his lover Io in the guise of a cloud.

▶ Jupiter and Io by Correggio

Leonardo da Vinci (1452–1519)

A true Renaissance man, Leonardo da Vinci was an inventor, artist, scientist, engineer, and architect.
He kept over 13,000 pages of journals with drawings on his observations of the world. He also drew designs for inventions—hang gliders, helicopters, war machines, bridges, musical instruments, water pumps, and much more. As a master of oil painting, da Vinci perfected the techniques of *chiaroscuro*, which is a way to use shadows to create 3-D effects. He was also known for *sfumato*, the use of slightly different shades of colour to move gently from light to dark. Both techniques can be seen in his most famous painting, the *Mona Lisa*.

▲ *A red chalk sketch of Leonardo da Vinci, thought to be a self-portrait from c.1512*

▲ *The Virgin of the Rocks places its figures in a pyramidical arrangement. Unlike most religious paintings set in golden light, it is painted in a mysterious, cave-like setting which showcases Leonardo's refined chiaroscuro*

▲ *Study of horses, c.1490*

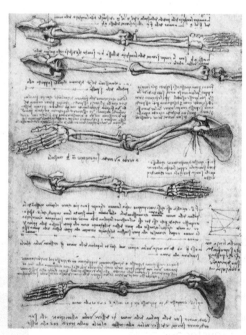

▲ *Leonardo's study of an arm shows how movement changes its shape*

A Perfectionist

Da Vinci strongly believed in bringing scientific observations into art. By his own count, Leonardo dissected 30 corpses in his lifetime! As a result, he had a deep understanding of muscles, bones, and organs in the body. He learned to match expressions such as smiling and frowning with the movement of facial muscles. This allowed him to make amazingly realistic drawings.

Saint Jerome in the Wilderness

Around 1482, Leonardo was going through a difficult time. He painted his inner turmoil into his most melancholic piece, *St. Jerome in the Wilderness*. The Christian saint fasted for years to purify his soul. Leonardo's unfinished painting shows a painfully thin man in a rocky desert. His face is twisted in suffering. His only companion is a lion, who stayed with the saint after he healed its paw.

 St. Jerome in the Wilderness shows Leonardo's humanism and his mastery over light and shade

The Last Supper

One of da Vinci's masterpieces is a mural called *The Last Supper*. It shows Christ and his disciples at the table. In the scene, the serene figure of Christ sits at the centre where he announces that one of his disciples will betray him. Da Vinci's painting shows the disciples taken aback in shock and disbelief. The artist began the painting around 1495. He carefully arranged and grouped the figures to balance each other out. However, each disciple reacts in a different way. Each person's thoughts and emotions are mirrored in his body language and expressions, as perceived by da Vinci. The painting is esteemed as a study of human emotions.

In Real Life

The Last Supper is not a true fresco, since it was not painted onto wet plaster. Because of this, the painting began to decay quickly. Although experts have restored the mural, little of its original paint remains.

▲ *Da Vinci's The Last Supper graces the wall of the Santa Maria delle Grazie in Milan, Italy*

The Mona Lisa (c.1503–1519)

The amazing *Mona Lisa* is believed to be a portrait of Lisa Gherardini, wife of a Florentine merchant. The painting showcases Leonardo's sfumato technique. The lines are soft and blurred, not sharp and clear. This gives the portrait a much more realistic look. Notice how soft shades, and not lines, create her lips, brows, face and fingers. The strokes of paint were applied in an irregular manner to make the grain of the skin appear more lifelike. Da Vinci played with light and shadows to create depth. It created the *Mona Lisa*'s most famous feature—her mysterious smile.

▶ *The Mona Lisa (also known as La Gioconda) is shown at the Louvre Museum in Paris*

Isn't It Amazing!

X-ray tests have shown that there are three older versions of the *Mona Lisa* under the present one! The painting was once stolen from the Louvre in Paris in 1911. However, the thief had trouble selling the painting that became famous due to the theft, and it was recovered two years later.

Michelangelo (1475-1564)

Nicknamed Il Divino (the divine one), Michelangelo di Lodovico Buonarroti Simoni was a painter, sculptor, architect, and engineer. He revolutionised Classical ideas about the human body. He believed that the plain, unrobed human body could express all emotions. He imbued his statues with muscle, movement, and incredible power. Such a use of nude figures greatly influenced Western artists of later times.

▲ *Madonna of Bruges, 1504*

▲ *The Crouching Boy, c.1530–1534*

▲ *Doni Tondo, c.1504–1506*

🏛 Apprentice Years

Michelangelo was born to a family of declining minor nobility. During his time, noblemen did not become artists as it was considered a step down. Thus, Michelangelo **apprenticed** at the somewhat late age of 13. He joined the workshop of Florence's famous Renaissance painter, Domenico Ghirlandaio. The talented teenager soon caught the attention of Lorenzo the Magnificent. He became a part of Lorenzo's household, where he met the greatest scholars of the era.

▲ *Battle of the Centaurs, 1492*

▲ *Bacchus, the Roman god of wine, one of Michelangelo's early sculptures, 1496–1497*

🏛 Pietà

When Lorenzo de' Medici passed away, Michelangelo was only about 17 years old. Yet, he travelled to Bologna and eventually reached Rome in 1496. Here, he made his great masterpiece, the *Pietà*. The sculpture shows the Virgin Mary grieving over Christ's body. It shows the artist's deep understanding of composition. He moulded the block of stone to show various contrasts—man and woman, vertical and horizontal, dead and alive, clothed and bare.

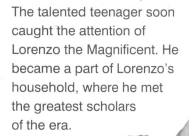
◄ *Pietà, 1498–1499*

David

In 1501, Michelangelo began his next masterpiece. For Florence's cathedral, he created the gigantic marble statue *David*, using geometrical formulae from Classical times. He did not however make the statue perfectly symmetrical. This made *David* truer to life. The statue is often considered an ideal form of humanity.

Incredible Individuals

Michelangelo is the first Western artist whose biography was published while he was still alive. It was written by artist and historian, Giorgio Vasari. Unfortunately, Michelangelo did not like it. So, he had his assistant Ascanio Condivi write a new one.

◄ *The statue of David, 1501–1504*

Michelangelo in Rome

In 1505, Pope Julius II commissioned Michelangelo to build him a magnificent tomb. The original plan had over 40 statues. But the design had to be scaled down eventually. The marble Moses on the tomb represents an imposing and important figure in religion. Michelangelo also made two other sculptures of slaves for the tomb. But he gave these to Roberto Strozzi, who took them to France and presented them to the king.

▲ *Moses for the tomb of Pope Julius II*

▲ *The Rebellious Slave and Dying Slave, which Michelangelo gave away*

The Last Judgement

In 1534, Michelangelo made a grandiose fresco for Pope Paul III. It shows Christ the Judge surrounded by saints, apostles and martyrs. Some souls are saved, some are damned. Towards the bottom, Charon the boatman ferries souls to hell, a scene from Classical mythology.

▶ *The Last Judgement, on the altar wall of the Sistine Chapel*

The Sistine Chapel

The Apostolic Palace is the official home of the Pope in the Vatican City. Here, the Pope's chapel is named the Sistine Chapel. It was built for Pope Sixtus IV (thus, the name Sistine) by the Renaissance architect, Giovanni dei Dolci. While the building looks plain from the outside, it is richly decorated inside with frescoes and tapestries. The most breathtaking sight is the ceiling, which was painted by Michelangelo. Of these paintings, the scenes from the *Book of Genesis* are the artist's most recognisable work.

Pattern on the Walls

The paintings on the walls are arranged in three sections. The lowest portion has tapestries of gold and silver designed by Raphael, depicting events from the Gospels. The middle tier is painted in two series, the life of Moses along the southern wall and the life of Christ along the northern. The uppermost portion depicts portraits of the popes.

▲ *The tiered paintings on the walls of the Sistine Chapel*

Early Frescoes

A number of Florence's early Renaissance masters decorated the Sistine Chapel. These included Michelangelo's teacher Domenico Ghirlandaio, Botticelli, Cosimo Rosselli, and Luca Signorelli. The Umbrian artists Perugino (c.1450–1523) and Pinturicchio (c.1454–1513) also added their frescoes.

▲ *Crossing of the Red Sea by Rosselli, 1481–1482*

▲ *Ceiling of the Sistine Chapel with the Genesis frescoes. The Last Judgement appears on the far wall*

Ceiling Fresco

In 1508, Pope Julius II (Sixtus IV's nephew) commissioned Michelangelo to paint the **barrel-vaulted** ceiling of the Sistine Chapel. Michelangelo took four years to complete the frescoes. He painted each part of the ceiling while carefully balanced on a high platform. He used a plaster mixture called **intonaco**. This gave the paintings a brighter colour and made them more visible from the floor far below. The entire ceiling is covered with the Genesis frescoes. They are a sequence of nine images of the creation of the world, stories of Adam and Eve, and stories of Noah. The prophets and sibyls who foretold the birth of Christ are painted at the sides.

▶ *The Separation of Light from Darkness*

The Flood

Michelangelo began by painting tales of Noah over the entrance. He then moved towards the altar, painting the stories in the opposite sequence. The scene of the Great Deluge shows Noah's Ark in the background. Noah and the other survivors are safely aboard while the rest of humanity struggles frantically to find a place of safety against the rising flood.

◀ *From the Noah series, the Flood*

Michelangelo's Genius

The first figures and scenes that Michelangelo drew on the ceiling were careful, small and stable. As he painted some more, he grew more confident. He worked faster. The figures became bolder with free movements and complex expressions. All the figures show the colossal strength that is a hallmark of Michelangelo's work. The ceiling is special because it shows both the heroic and tragic tales of humanity.

▶ *In the Last Judgement fresco, Michelangelo painted St. Bartholomew with his own flayed skin in hand*

▲ *Painting of a Libyan Sibyl*

Adam and Eve

Michelangelo took a year-long break while painting the ceiling, and the frescoes show this passage of time as there is a strong emotionality in the later frescoes that is missing from the earlier ones. The next work, *The Creation of Adam*, is monumental and suffused with emotion. It is Michelangelo's most famous piece. The entire scene shows a thoughtful restraint, making this one of the most expressive masterworks of the Renaissance.

▲ *The Creation of Eve*

▲ *The Creation of Adam*

Raphael (1483–1520)

Master painter and architect of the High Renaissance, Raphael is best known for his work in the Vatican. He is also famous for his many paintings of the Madonna. Though his life was short, his days were full of activity and he left behind many amazing pieces of art. He even ran a large workshop and was one of the most influential artists of Rome.

▲ Raphael's magnificent La Disputa was painted for Pope Julius II's room. It shows God, the prophets, and the apostles above a gathering of the Roman Catholic Church, representing the triumph of the Church

▲ The Triumph of Galatea (1511) is Raphael's more secular and mythology-oriented work

Early Years

Raphael was born in Urbino, in Italy. His father, the painter Giovanni Santi, was his first teacher. However, Giovanni passed away when his son was only 11. Raphael then joined the workshop of the great Umbrian master Pietro Perugino. Here, he picked up a great deal of professional knowledge. He was also influenced by Perugino's quietly exquisite style. Perugino's *Christ Handing the Keys to St. Peter* (1482) inspired Raphael's first major piece, *The Marriage of the Virgin* (1504).

▲ Raphael's The Marriage of the Virgin

▲ Perugino's Christ Handing the Keys to St. Peter, a fresco in the Sistine Chapel

The Young Master

By 1500, the young Raphael was already a master in his own right. His expertise can be seen in an altarpiece that he helped paint in 1502. Around the same time, he painted an important piece called *Coronation of the Virgin* for the Oddi Chapel. This is the first of many paintings that tells a story. Others from a few years later include *Vision of a Knight*, *St. George and the Dragon*, *Three Graces,* and *St. Michael*. Each piece is done with youthful freshness yet shows the artist's skill and control.

▶ The Coronation of the Virgin shows the empty tomb of Mary, who has been raised to Heaven and crowned by Christ

▲ *St. George and the Dragon and St. Michael Overwhelming the Demon show Raphael's budding interest in martial subjects*

▲ *Painted much later in life, this second St. Michael Vanquishing Satan shows the artist's more mature work on the same subject*

 ## The Florentine Madonna

By 1504, Raphael was in Florence and learning from the works of great Renaissance artists. He was particularly influenced by Leonardo da Vinci's *sfumato*, which is the use of soft shading (instead of lines) to create forms. However, Raphael went further in creating new types of figures. Also, while Leonardo and Michelangelo painted intense and dark emotions, Raphael painted gentler expressions. The most important work of this time is a series of Madonnas. It includes the *Madonna of the Goldfinch* (c.1505), *Madonna of the Meadow* (c.1500–1506), *Esterházy Madonna* (c.1503–1508) and *La Belle Jardinière* (c.1507).

▶ *In The Deposition (1507), Raphael explored the techniques of Michelangelo to depict the strength of human figures, while developing his own storytelling style*

 ## The Rome Madonna

The later Madonnas of Raphael are more energetic in movement. This can be seen in the sophisticated pose of the *Alba Madonna* (1510). The *Madonna di Foligno* (1511–1512) and the *Sistine Madonna* (1513) are richly coloured and more grandiose in composition.

◀ *The Liberation of St. Peter, in the Stanza d'Eliodoro room, is a night scene. It is unique for using three forms of light—a torch, the moonlight and supernatural light from an angel*

⊛ Incredible Individuals

In 1508, Pope Julius II called Raphael to Rome. Raphael's personality, charm, and artistic talent made him immensely popular. Giorgio Vasari dubbed him the 'Prince of Painters'.

▶ *A self-portrait, around age 23*

The School of Athens

Among Raphael's most famous paintings is the *School of Athens.* It shows the ancient Greek philosophers Plato and Aristotle striding forward in discussion. Famous poets, mathematicians, dramatists, philosophers, and leaders of the past surround them. These are symbols of human knowledge, who represent the birth of new ideas.

 ## Stanza della Segnatura

The *School of Athens* adorns one wall of the Stanza della Segnatura in the Vatican. The Pope worked in this room. It was originally meant to be his library. Thus, Raphael painted it with frescoes that inspire thought and reflection. On the opposite wall is the equally amazing *Disputa*, which symbolises religious faith and practice. Raphael also painted the two remaining walls. These showcase smaller frescoes called the *Parnassus* (which symbolises literature) and the *Cardinal Virtues*. Altogether, the paintings show contrasting religious and secular beliefs.

▲ *The Stanza della Segnatura with the School of Athens on the wall to the right*

▲ *The School of Athens with Plato and Aristotle at the centre*

 ## Portraits

Raphael painted the historic figures with some well-known Renaissance faces. The tall central figure of Plato, with his flowing beard and hair, is thought to be a portrait of Leonardo da Vinci. The philosopher Heraclitus is seen sitting on his own, brooding. His figure is believed to be inspired from Michelangelo, who had a similar brooding nature. Raphael used this overlap of past and present figures on purpose. He meant to show how the Classical masters and the Renaissance greats held shared beliefs.

▲ *Michelangelo as Heraclitus*

▲ *Identified as the mathematician Euclid, the bent figure in red robes is thought to be a portrait of the great Renaissance architect Donato Bramante*

Plato & Aristotle

The two main figures in the work are clearly Plato and Aristotle. They are placed under the main archway and at a distance which automatically draws your eye to them. This is a deliberate play on perspective by Raphael. The two men stand for two different schools of philosophy. The elderly Plato points a finger to the sky. He believes that the "real" world is not physical but spiritual and abstract. His student Aristotle throws his arm out towards the viewer. Aristotle believes that knowledge comes from observation and experience of the physical realm. The various other scholars are arranged on either side of Plato and Aristotle, depending on each man's beliefs.

 ## Socrates

The brilliant Greek philosopher Socrates stands to the left of Plato. Raphael painted him using an ancient bust for reference. He is cloaked in a long robe. He holds up his hand in a gesture that is considered characteristic of the philosopher. The group that he is addressing consists of his most famous students, General Alcibiades and the philosopher Aeschines. Some experts believe that the figure of Alcibiades is in fact Alexander the Great.

▲ *Socrates with his students. The womanly figure below them is thought to be Hypatia. She was a wise mathematician, philosopher, and teacher of ancient Greece*

 ## Pythagoras

The genius Greek mathematician Pythagoras is the centre of another group. He sits holding a large open book and inkpot. Looking attentively over his shoulder is Ibn Rushd, more popularly known as Averroës, the brilliant Muslim polymath and philosopher.

▶ *Pythagoras and Averroës*

👤 In Real Life

Like many modern scientists, Pythagoras believed in both science and spirituality. Though grounded in mathematics, he believed that upon death, the immortal soul was reborn in a new body.

Renaissance in Venice

The Quattrocento was a significant period for Venice. The city was located at the crossroads between the Byzantine East and the Gothic West. It was wealthy, well connected, and had a successful government headed by the Doge (dukes). After the fall of Constantinople in 1453, Venice attracted the brilliant minds of the Christian and Arabic East. It also attracted Renaissance masters from Europe. As a result, the Venetian Renaissance was an amazing mix of cultural forces.

▲ Carpaccio's rich and bustling court scene is the second painting from the St. Ursula series of wall paintings in Venice

▲ Renaissance portrait by Lazzaro Bastiani of Francesco Foscari, who was the Doge of Venice from 1423 till 1457

 ## Venetian Trends

While Florence focused on composition and shading, Rome addressed dramatic movement and Venice perfected the use of colour. Perhaps, the last was inspired by the sea and by the network of canals that ran through Venice. From the time of Vittore Carpaccio (c.1460–1525), painters tried to capture the dazzling lights reflected onto the buildings and bridges. Artists drew bustling landscapes of 15th century Venice, with its *gondolas* (rowboats), festivals and religious processions.

▲ The *Miracle of the True Cross at the Bridge of San Lorenzo* by Gentile Bellini

▲ In the Arrival of the Pilgrims, a 1490 painting from the Legend of St. Ursula series, Carpaccio shows Attila the Hun, who has taken over the city, being informed of Ursula and the pilgrims' arrival

 ## The Bellini Family

Venetian Renaissance was founded by Jacopo Bellini (c. 1400–1470) and his sons Gentile (c.1429–1507) and Giovanni (c.1430–1516). The Bellini's huge workshop received many patrons and taught many artists. Giovanni was one of the first here to adopt the Flemish technique of oil painting. His works focus on naturalism. He united the Italian attention to anatomy with the Dutch sense of realism. His skill with oil painting techniques created incredible depth and glow while giving an almost photographic realism to his paintings.

◀ Giovanni's portrait of Doge Leonardo Loredan is realistic and forceful. The artist rejected the early Renaissance manner of painting profiles. Instead he chose a three-quarter view of the subject

▲ Gentile Bellini spent a year at the Ottoman court and painted amazing portraits like that of Sultan Mehmet II in 1480

▲ Gentile's *Procession of the True Cross in the Piazza San Marco* shows Venice in the late 1400s

Giorgione (c.1477–1510)

Giorgione was a master at colouring. His most famous piece is *The Tempest* (see p. 15). His *Three Philosophers* is a skilful expression of light. It shows the three ages of man. The three men are thought to represent different philosophical movements: ancient thought, Arabic philosophy, and the Renaissance.

▶ *The Three Philosophers, 1508–1509*

Titian (c.1490–1576)

A celebrity artist, Titian painted amazing landscapes with intimate groups of people. His *Noli me Tangere* shows the Garden of Gethsemane, where Mary mistakes Christ for a gardener. Against this gentle backdrop stands the risen Christ warning Mary Magdalene not to touch him, because he is soon to ascend to heaven, and he doesn't want his followers to get attached to his physical being. The figures express intense emotion.

▶ *Titian's self-portrait*

▲ Tintoretto sacrificed naturalism and used distorted forms and colours to communicate strong feelings and a supernatural eventfulness in the *Last Supper*

▲ In the *Transportation of the Body of St Mark*, Tintoretto uses a diagonal composition that pulls the viewer's eye at an angle from figure to figure

Tintoretto (1518–1594)

Jacopo Robusti, called Tintoretto, was the last of Venice's Renaissance masters, and also a revered Mannerist painter of the Venetian school. Tintoretto composed paintings with an eye for the effect created by light and space.

Mannerism

Mannerism arose during the later years of the Renaissance. The Italian word *maniera* means manner or style. Mannerist art is a bridge between the High Renaissance and the ornate Baroque art that followed it. It began in Florence and Rome, and then spread to the rest of Europe. It remained highly popular until artists such as Annibale Carracci and Caravaggio revived Naturalism and brought Mannerism to an end.

▶ *Caravaggio paints the calling of St. Mathew realistically, with stark lighting and without angels or any supernatural elements. It marks the end of Mannerism and the beginnings of Baroque*

Mannerist Painting

Mannerism came about as a reaction to the Classical and idealised styles of the Renaissance. Ignoring some of the strict Renaissance rules of harmony and proportion, Mannerism is a less natural and more exaggerated form of art. For instance, human figures are made much longer than normal and painted in artificial poses. The lighting and colours were often bold to the point of garish. Sometimes, early Mannerism pieces (c.1520–1535) were even called anti-Classical. Later, it developed into High Mannerism (c.1535–1580), which is a more intricate and meditative style. High Mannerism art was often created for sophisticated and wealthy patrons of art.

▲ *Pontormo's Deposition from the Cross shows a mass of people in a flat space. The necks and bodies are exaggerated, twisted, and stretched in various poses*

▲ *Rosso Fiorentino's Deposition from the Cross, shows angular figures and hurried movements, set in an almost geometric design*

Mannerist Artists

Elements of Mannerism can be seen in the later works of Michelangelo, Raphael, and Correggio. Other Renaissance artists such as Rosso Fiorentino and Jacopo da Pontormo also broke away from Classicism and began indulging in Mannerist styles. They painted long limbs, small heads, stylised expressions, and agitated emotions. Followers of Raphael, like Giulio Romano and Polidoro da Caravaggio, also emerged as Mannerist artists.

◀ *Giulio Romano's Fall of the Giants creates the illusion of a dome. In the centre, Jupiter sends grotesque giants crashing down with thunderbolts for daring to invade Mt. Olympus*

The Sack of Rome

On 6 May 1527, armies of the Holy Roman Emperor Charles V stormed through Rome, looting and killing everything in sight. This brought an end to the Renaissance movement in the city. Artists of the new Mannerist movement fled for their lives. They took the style to other parts of Italy and Europe. Among them were Francesco Salviati, Domenico Beccafumi, Federico Zuccari, and Pellegrino Tibaldi. The most important of them was Bronzino, who became the greatest Mannerist painter in Florence at the time. The Dutch cities of Haarlem and Amsterdam welcomed the new style. In Prague, Emperor Rudolf II became its most ambitious patron.

▲ *Fire Sent Down from Heaven by Beccafumi (1538–1539) at the Pisa Cathedral*

▲ *Haarlem-based Hendrik Goltzius was one of the most technically skilled Mannerists. See his sophisticated use of lighting and detail in Sine Cerere et Baccho friget Venus (Without Ceres and Bacchus, Venus would freeze)*

Parmigianino (1503–1540)

The Italian artist Girolamo Francesco Maria Mazzola is better known as Parmigianino. He was one of the earliest and most influential Mannerist artists. Parmigianino himself was deeply influenced by Correggio. This can be seen in his first important piece, the *Mystic Marriage of St. Catherine* (c.1521). His Mannerist art was characterised by icy lighting, distorted spaces, and unnaturally long forms. All these elements give his works a strange emotional intensity. After the sack of Rome, Parmigianino left for Bologna and then Parma, where he created masterpieces like the *Madonna with the Long Neck*.

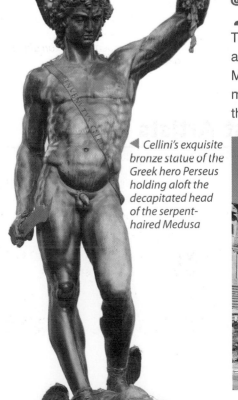

◀ *Cellini's exquisite bronze statue of the Greek hero Perseus holding aloft the decapitated head of the serpent-haired Medusa*

▶ *Madonna with the Long Neck (c.1534) shows the elongated features that are a hallmark of Mannerism*

Sculpture

The sculptors Bartolomeo Ammannati and Benvenuto Cellini made extraordinary Mannerist sculptures. However, perhaps the most complex and graceful statues come from the Mannerist master Giambologna.

◀ *Florence's famous Fountain of Neptune, designed by Bartolomeo Ammannati in 1565*

El Greco (1541–1614)

The Greek-born Doménikos Theotokópoulos was a master of Spanish painting during the Mannerist period. His paintings were so far ahead of his time, they left many of his contemporaries puzzled. It was only in the 20th century that his art came to be really understood. He also worked as a sculptor and architect. While he was living in Italy, he was given the name by which he became famous, El Greco (The Greek). He never forgot his Greek origins and always signed his work using his full and original name.

◀ The Agony in the Garden of Gethsemane, c.1590, shows Christ and an angel against a foreboding background. The apostles are asleep in a cocoon, while in the distance Judas approaches with soldiers

◀ The Vision of St. John (1608–1614) shows how markedly different El Greco's art was from Renaissance art. It is said to have inspired the 20th century genius Picasso to paint Les Demoiselles d'Avignon (The Young Ladies of Avignon)

Expressionism

El Greco's highly individual and dramatic style makes him neither a Renaissance painter nor a true Mannerist. Indeed, his work is closer to the Expressionism style of much later centuries. El Greco is best known for his religious paintings. These show long, tortured-looking figures on unnaturally coloured backdrops. The paintings are a mix of eastern (Byzantine-Greek) and western styles. The intensely spiritual result was very attractive to the Catholic Church of Spain. Thus, El Greco was welcomed with open arms to the country.

El Greco's paintings are often tumultuous, with a rhythm like the broken waves of a sea. Light seems to emanate from within the characters that adds drama to the art.

▲ The Adoration of the Name of Jesus is a great example of the themes El Greco usually explored

▲ El Greco's art was unlike anything ever seen in or before the Mannerist period. His Baptism of Christ is one such example

Rejecting the Renaissance

In the 1560s, El Greco went to study art in Venice. He joined the studio of Titian, who was then the greatest painter in Italy. El Greco naturally studied the works of the Renaissance masters, particularly those of Michelangelo, Raphael, and Titian. Yet, he refused to submit to their artistic beliefs. He believed in his own talent and was determined to create his own form of art. This was easier to do away from Italy. Thus, in 1577, he moved to Toledo, Spain.

▶ *The Penitent Magdalene, one of the first works painted in Toledo, shows Titian's influence on El Greco*

Spain and Fame

El Greco made a name for himself when he did a set of paintings for the church of Santo Domingo el Antiguo in Toledo. He then created two pieces for Philip II of Spain, the *Allegory of the Holy League* and *Martyrdom of St. Maurice*, in 1580–1582. Unfortunately, the king did not like the latter painting, and El Greco was no longer associated with the Spanish court. In 1586, he painted the amazing *Burial of the Count de Orgaz* which soon became his most famous work. Over time, El Greco's paintings became less descriptive and more dramatic. He drew the human body taller and paler.

El Greco's Painting

The almost violent way in which El Greco painted his pieces shows an early form of Expressionism. They are far from the Realism and Naturalism that were popular with artists and patrons of his time. Most important in his work is his use of light. Many of his figures seem to be lit from within. Sometimes, they reflect a light from some unknown source. The flashes of light give way to swirls of gloomily clad figures, half-hidden threats and distorted gestures. Each painting is a thrilling puzzle of emotions.

▲ *Burial of the Count of Orgaz, 1586*

◀ *The Assumption of the Virgin, one of the paintings at Santo Domingo el Antiguo that made El Greco famous*

Isn't It Amazing!

El Greco said of Michelangelo that he was a "good man, but he did not know how to paint." Despite this, Michelangelo has a strong influence on some of El Greco's works, such as *The Holy Trinity*.

▲ *The View of Toledo is one of two surviving landscapes of the city painted by El Greco*

Word Check

Ancient & Medieval Architecture

Abaton: It refers to an ancient Greek enclosure in the temple of Asclepios where patients slept.

Adobe: It is clay-like material used for building structures.

Amphitheatre: It is a circular building with rising levels of seating (as seen in a football stadium).

Arabesques: It is an intricate floral pattern, sometimes with animals and figures included.

Arcade: It is an arched, covered passageway or gallery.

Barracks: It is a place where soldiers are housed.

Calligraphy: The art of beautiful handwriting.

Caravanserai: It is an Eastern hotel with overnight parking space for caravans.

Confucian: A person who believes in the teachings of the Chinese philosopher Confucius.

Corbels: It is a structure that sticks out from a wall and supports weight.

Crenellated: It is a defensive wall into which gaps (crenels) are added. The gaps were used to bombard enemy soldiers with missiles.

Filigreed: Delicate ornamental work made of fine wire.

Gypsum: It is a material used in the making of plaster of Paris and drywall.

Hieroglyph: An image of an object representing a word.

Iconography: It describes the images and symbols that are associated with religious and legendary figures.

Mausoleum: It is a building that houses one or more tombs.

Mosaics: They are decorations made by putting together different coloured tiles to form a pattern.

Motley: Consisting of different types, parts, or colours that don't seem to fit together.

Nabatean: It is an ancient Arab kingdom.

Pastoral: It is related to the open green countryside; rural, not urban.

Pedestal: It is the base or foot of a column.

Pharaohs: Ancient Egypt's rulers who were the political and religious heads of the state.

Porphyry: It is a large rock containing crystals of quartz or feldspar.

Roundels: It is a round object, like a window or a decorative plate.

Ventilation: It is a system for providing fresh air.

Ancient & Medieval Art

Abbot: A man who is in charge of an abbey of monks.

Amphora: It is a long oval jar or vase with a narrow cylindrical neck and two large handles.

Bodhisattva: One who undertakes Buddhist practices that can lead them to enlightenment.

Caliph: It was a title used by powerful Muslim rulers of medieval times.

Ceramics: They are clay pots that are hardened by heat, usually painted, glazed, or coloured.

Enamel: It is a glassy substance that is fused to metal (or other materials) under high heat, to give brightly coloured, glossy effects.

Equinox: Twice a year, the Sun lies directly above the equator. This is called the equinox. During the equinox, people on the equator experience equal hours of day and night.

Fresco: It is a type of mural (wall painting) in which colour is applied to wet plaster on a wall. As it dries, the wall absorbs the paint and makes it long-lasting.

Lacquer: It is a hard, shiny substance applied to wooden objects to give them a polished look.

Lapis lazuli: It is a deep blue semi-precious stone.

Mosaic: It is a form of art where the image is made by sticking together tiny pieces of coloured glass, clay, stone or other materials.

Opaque: It is an object that prevents light from travelling through, and is therefore not transparent or translucent.

Relief sculpture: They are the carvings that are made into a solid surface, like a wall or a stone slab.

Seals: They are stamps made of clay, wax, stone, or other materials. They were used to seal and stamp important documents in older times.

Standard: It is a banner or flag whose design stands for an important person or institution.

Stele: It is a tall wooden or stone slab, carved, and erected as a boundary stone, grave marker, or in memory of an important event.

Veneer: It is a thin sheet of superior wood, porcelain, or other material. It is used to cover and protect another object, like a piece of furniture.

Modern Architecture

Age of Reason: It is also called the Age of Enlightenment; this was an intellectual and philosophical movement in 18th century Europe.

Arabesque: It is a form of decoration made of scrolling, interlacing tendrils, foliage or plain lines.

Baltic States: It is the combined name for three independent nations on the eastern coast of the Baltic Sea—Estonia, Latvia, and Lithuania.

Brick Expressionism: A style of architecture that used bricks and tiles; it existed during the 1920s around Germany and the Netherlands.

Byzantine: It is anything relating to Byzantium, a Christian empire of medieval times that centred on the city of Constantinople, which is now modern-day Istanbul.

Cossack Hetmanate: 'Cossack' means 'free man' and 'Hetman' means 'headman'. The Cossack Hetmanate was the government of an independent 17th or 18th century nation that became modern Ukraine.

Curtain wall: On a building, this is an outer layer of any material (stone or glass or iron) that carries only its own weight. It is often used for decorative impact.

Hellenist: It is anything relating to ancient Greek culture, especially between 4th–1st century BCE.

Manueline: It is a lavish, decorative style of architecture that existed in Portugal during the 16th century during (and just after) the reign of King Manuel I.

Ottoman Empire: Between the 14th and 20th centuries, great swathes of southeast Europe, northwest Asia, and northern Africa were controlled by Turkish emperors called the Ottomans.

Reinforced concrete: It is concrete that is reinforced by another material, usually steel bars embedded into the concrete.

Relief: It is a sculpture that is attached to walls so that it rises from or above the wall surface.

Renaissance: It refers to the period of revival of Classical (ancient Greek and Roman) art and architecture during the 14th to 16th centuries. It began in Italy and spread to the rest of Europe.

Paternoster: In buildings, a paternoster is a type of lift with many open compartments travelling up and down on a conveyor-belt-like mechanism. The compartments do not stop at the floor, but they travel slowly, so you can just jump off at the right floor, while it keeps moving upwards/downwards.

Stucco: It is a fine plaster that is used to coat walls or sometimes mould into decorative forms.

Turreted: A building that has a turret (a small tower on top of a larger tower or building).

Modern Art

Allegory: It is the illustration of ideas and concepts like love, revolution, glory, etc., in the form of symbols and human figures.

Avant-garde: It is a French word for 'advance guard'; it refers to artists who are at the forefront of radical and ground-breaking new styles.

Chiaroscuro: It is a style of painting that contrasts dark and light colours, usually to enhance the three-dimensional effect of a painting.

Contrapposto: It is an Italian word that describes a human pose. It is when the figure stands with most of its body weight on one leg, while the other leg is free and bent a little at the knee. The upper part of the body is usually angled in a natural way.

Easels: They are the wooden frames that hold the artist's canvas.

Great Depression: It was a severe worldwide economic crisis in the 1930s that robbed people of their homes and their livelihood.

Impasto: It is a way of painting in which the paint is applied in such thick layers, with a brush or painting knife, that it sticks out of the canvas.

Palette: It is a board on which the painter can mix colours before applying them to the canvas.

Tenebrism: It is a style of painting developed by 17th century Spanish and Italian painters (notably Caravaggio). It makes use of dark shadows to paint a picture while highlighting selected parts.

Renaissance Architecture

Apse: It is a semi-circular room-like space that is covered with a hemispherical dome.

Bays: It is the space distinguished by vertical lines or planes, i.e. elements like columns.

Blind arches: It is an arch decorating a solid wall, instead of opening into a window or passage.

Burghers: They were the privileged citizens of European towns who were often elected to some governing role.

Cloister: It is a covered walkway, usually in the form of a quadrangle, along the wall of a convent, college, or monastery.

Cupola: It is a rounded dome that

forms the ceiling of a building.

Drums: Also called tholobates, they are the cylindrical stone blocks which make up the upright part of a building on which a dome is raised. They are generally in the shape of a cylinder or a polygonal prism.

Garrison: It is a body of troops stationed in a particular location.

High Renaissance: It is the period when the Renaissance influence was at its highest point.

Illuminated manuscripts: They are medieval texts with miniature paintings and decorations in gold or silver.

Loggia: It is a gallery or room with open sides that looks out onto a garden or some other scenery.

Pilaster: A rectangular column that projects from the wall.

Prodigy houses: Showy mansions built during the Elizabethan and Jacobean era.

Relief: They are carvings that are raised from a solid surface, like a wall.

Renaissance: It is the period between the 14th and 17th century in Europe when there was a surge in the rediscovery of art, architecture, literature, and philosophy.

Roundels: It is a small disc or decorative medallion.

Serliana openings: It is also called a Palladian or Venetian window; a three-part window made of a large, arched central section bordered by two narrower sections having square tops.

Renaissance Art

Anatomy: It is the structure of a living being, including the relative position and function of all parts.

Annunciation: It is the moment when the archangel Gabriel tells Mary that she will become the mother of Christ.

Apprentice: This refers to a person who acquires skills from a master for a period of time for low wages.

Baptistery: It is the part of the church where the ritual of baptism is held.

Barrel-vaulted: It describes a ceiling that is curved in a half cylinder like a barrel.

Bust: It is a sculpture of the upper part of a human being, from head to chest.

Condottiere: It is a soldier who could be hired for money, which was a common practice in 15th century Europe.

Draughtsman: It is a person who draws accurately with technical mastery.

Humanism: It is the belief that the needs and values of human beings supersede religious dogma.

Intonaco: It is an Italian word for the thin layer of plaster on which an artist paints a fresco. The painting is created while the plaster is wet so that the pigment penetrates into it.

Patron: It refers to a person who supports an artist or writer by paying for their works and supporting their livelihood.

Polyptych: It is an artwork that is made up of a number of attached panels.

Renaissance: It refers to the period between the 14th and 16th centuries, when there was a revival of European scholarship and art under the influence of Classical models.

Sfumato: It is a form in painting where there are no clear lines. Instead, form is created by shading or blending colours.

Surreal: It means that something seems fantastic or unbelievable in a dream-like manner.

Symbolism: It is a method of using symbols to represent an idea or quality. Symbolism also refers to an artistic movement where people used symbolic images or ideas to convey their emotions, mystical ideas or state of mind.

Three-dimensional: It refers to objects that have length, breadth and height. It is also simply called 3D. Paintings can be thought of as two-dimensional (2D), because they have no real height. Thus, artists use various tricks and techniques of perspective to show us real-life 3D objects on 2D paper.

Trompe-l'œil: It is the style of painting that creates the illusion of three dimensions.

a: above, b: below/ bottom, c: centre, f: far, l: left, r: right, t: top, bg: background

Cover

Shutterstock: Back: Mountains Hunter; Tymonko Galyna;

Wikimedia Commons: Front: File:5 Estancia del Sello (La Disputa del Sacramento).jpg / https://commons.wikimedia.org/wiki/File:5_Estancia_del_Sello_(La_Disputa_del_Sacramento).jpg; File:Vincent van Gogh - Wheatfield with crows - Google Art Project.jpg / https://commons.wikimedia.org/wiki/File:Vincent_van_Gogh_-_Wheatfield_with_crows_-_Google_Art_Project.jpg Back: File:Ajanta Padmapani.jpg / https://commons.wikimedia.org/wiki/File:Ajanta_Padmapani.jpg; File:Giorgio Vasari - The Last Judgment - WGA24313.jpg / https://commons.wikimedia.org/wiki/File:Giorgio_Vasari_-_The_Last_Judgment_-_WGA24313.jpg; File:Saints Peter and Paul Cathedral in Peterhof 01.jpg / https://commons.wikimedia.org/wiki/File:Saints_Peter_and_Paul_Cathedral_in_Peterhof_01.jpg

Ancient & Medieval Architecture

Inside

Shutterstock: 3background/tan_tan; 3b/pinholeimaging; 4tr/Emiliano Pane; 4b/De steve estvanik; 5cl/Khaled ElAdawy; 5br/cineuno; 6 & 7 b/Kirill Skorobogatko; 7tl/Jawwad Ali; 7cr/suronin; 8tl/Graficam Ahmed Saeed; 8tc/Kokhanchikov; 8tr/Tomas Nevesely; 8cr/Leksi.photo; 8bl/Mountains Hunter; 8 &9b/WitR; 9tr/Sompol; 9c/Pakhnyushchy; 10tl/mountainpix; 10tr/Borisb17; 10cr/Cara-Foto; 10bl/anyaivanova; 10br/Tymonko Galyna; 11cr/Georgios Tsichlis; 11br/Anton Chygarev; 12cl/Benny Marty; 12cr/Phant; ; 12& 13 b/De Phant; 13cl/John Copland; 13cr/muratart; 13br/JopsStock; 14tl/Rangzen; 14cl/Nejron Photo; 14 & 15 b/Filip Fuxa; 15tr/Baturina Yuliya; 16tl/Nicha; 16tr/Mark Brandon; 16 & 17 b/zhao jiankang; 17tr/zhao jiankang; 17cl/pinholeimaging; 17cr/Lekchalit; 17bl/qian; 18tl/Martin Froyda; 18cr/Barone Firenze; 18c/wong yu liang; 18 & 19b/kavalenkau; 19tc/Jan-Dirk Hansen; 19tr/Mikadun; 19cr/YURY TARANIK; 19cl/Ruslan Kalnitsky; 20tr/Dmitry Rukhlenko; 20bl/Michal Knitl; 21tr/Dmitry Rukhlenko; 21cl/Radiokafka; 21cr/Shal09; 22tl/Sean Pavone; 22br/AINI SYAHIZA; 23tl/Guitar photographer; 23c/Jak149; 23b/Efired; 24tl/Jon Chica; 24bl/Vichy Deal; 25tr/M88; 25tl/Thanaporn Pinpart; 25cl/Filip Fuxa; 25c/Shuosong; 25br/RAYphotographer; 26tr/I and S Walker; 26cl/IR Stone; 27tr/Walkabout Photo Guides; 27cl/spacaj; 27br/Anton_Ivanov; 28tr/Pavlov Valeriy; 28cr/Catarina Belova; 28 & 29b/NatureStock1; 29c/Benny Marty; 30tl/Suchart Boonyavech; 30tc/Frank Bach; 30tr/zebra0209; 30cl/kompasstudio; 30c/Heather Shimmin; 30cr/Ure; 30br/Bill Perry; 31tr/aesthetic424; 31cr/PhilMacDPhoto; 31bl/elvistudio

Wikimedia Commons: 4tl/Poplar_Cottage_at_Weald_and_Down/Oast House Archive / Poplar Cottage at Weald & Downland Museum, Singleton, West Sussex/wikimedia commons; 4cl/Toda_Hut/Pratheep P S, www.pratheep.com / CC BY-SA (https://creativecommons.org/licenses/by-sa/3.0)/wikimedia commons; 5tr/Igloos/Charles Francis Hall / Public domain/wikimedia commons; 6tr/Реконструкця лодки у причала в Эриду на которых плавали в Урук.jpg/Таис Гило / Public domain/wikimedia commons; 6cl/John_Henry_Haynes._Nippur,_circa_1899/John Henry Haynes / Public domain/wikimedia commons; 6c/Mesopotamia_in_2nd_millennium_BC/Joeyhewitt / CC BY-SA (https://creativecommons.org/licenses/by-sa/3.0)/wikimedia commons; 6cr/Hanging_Gardens_of_Babylon/Maarten van Heemskerck / Public domain/wikimedia commons; 7br/20101229_Naqsh_e_Rostam_Shiraz_Iran_more_Panoramic/User:Ggia / CC BY-SA (https://creativecommons.org/licenses/by-sa/3.0)/wikimedia commons; 8br/File:Sakkara, la pyramide LCCN2017656975.tif/Photoglob Co., publisher / Public domain/wikimedia commons; 11tr/Artemis_Efes_Museum/Pvasiliadis / Public domain/wikimedia commons; 11tr/Templo-Artemisa-Efeso-2017/FDV / CC BY-SA (https://creativecommons.org/licenses/by-sa/4.0)/wikimedia commons; 15c/Lower_church_of_Saint_Basil_s_Cathedral_07/shakko / CC BY-SA (https://creativecommons.org/licenses/by-sa/3.0)/wikimedia commons; 20br/A_closeup_of_mandapa_above_a_Hindu_temple_Cave_16_Ellora_India/Jean-Pierre Dalbéra from Paris, France / CC BY (https://creativecommons.org/licenses/by/2.0)/wikimedia commons; 21cl/Chennakesava_Temple-Somanathapura/Vishwakiran / CC BY-SA (https://creativecommons.org/licenses/by-sa/4.0)/wikimedia commons; 21br/SUCHINDAM_(13)/Ssriram mt / CC BY-SA (https://creativecommons.org/licenses/by-sa/4.0)/wikimedia commons; 22tr/Temples_of_Thailand/Milei.vencel / CC BY-SA (https://creativecommons.org/licenses/by-sa/3.0)/wikimedia commons; 22cr/Sailendra_King_and_Queen,_Borobudur (1)/Gunawan Kartapranata / CC BY-SA (https://creativecommons.org/licenses/by-sa/3.0)/wikimedia commons; 22bc/File:COLLECTIE TROPENMUSEUM Reliëf O 89 op de verborgen voet van de Borobudur TMnr 10015826.jpg/Tropenmuseum / Public domain/wikimedia commons; 24cr/Sankeien_Choshukaku/Urashimataro / Public domain/wikimedia commons; 26bl/Mesaverde_cliffpalace_20030914.752 (1)/Lorax / CC BY-SA (http://creativecommons.org/licenses/by-sa/3.0/)/wikimedia commons; 28cl/Aachener1723aDom/Bojin / CC BY-SA (https://creativecommons.org/licenses/by-sa/3.0)/wikimedia commons; 29tl/Modillonsarthous2//wikimedia commons; 29cr/Saint-Savin-sur-Gartempe_(86)_Abbatiale_Interieur_02/GO69 / CC BY-SA (https://creativecommons.org/licenses/by-sa/3.0)/wikimedia commons; 30bl/Notre-Dame_Rzygacze/Krzysztof Mizera / CC BY-SA (https://creativecommons.org/licenses/by-sa/4.0)/wikimedia commons

Ancient & Medieval Art

Inside

Shutterstock: 3b/Erlantz P.R; 3background/tan_tan; 4tl/Kevin Standage; 4cl/Abdoabdalla; 5cr/buteo; 7b/Dima Moroz; 9br/SSSCCC; 10bl/OPIS Zagreb; 17br/Matteo Gabrieli; 16tr1/Lefteris Papaulakis; 18cl/Travel Stock; 22tr/Ke Wang

Wikimedia Commons: 4cr/Venus_of_Willendorf_frontview_retouched_2/User:MatthiasKabel / CC BY-SA (http://creativecommons.org/licenses/by-sa/3.0/)/wikimedia commons; 4cr/F07_0054.Ma/Jochen Jahnke / CC BY-SA (http://creativecommons.org/licenses/by-sa/3.0/)/wikimedia commons; 4br/Prehistoric_Rock_Paintings_at_Manda_Gu,li_Cave_in_the_Ennedi_Mountains_-_northeastern_Chad_2015/David Stanley from Nanaimo, Canada / CC BY (https://creativecommons.org/licenses/by/2.0)/wikimedia commons; 5tl/File:Altamira bisons.jpg/Thomas Quine / CC BY-SA (https://creativecommons.org/licenses/by-sa/2.0)/wikimedia commons; 5tr/Sleeping_Antelope_Tin_Taghirt/Linus Wolf / CC BY-SA (https://creativecommons.org/licenses/by-sa/3.0)/wikimedia commons; 5bl/Bedollina_roccia_1_foto_rilievo/Luparch / CC BY-SA (https://creativecommons.org/licenses/by-sa/3.0)/wikimedia commons; 6tr/File:Mesopotamia male worshiper 2750-2600 B.C.jp/Rosemaniakos from Bejing (hometown) / CC BY-SA (https://creativecommons.org/licenses/by-sa/2.0)/wikimedia commons; 6c/Stele_of_Vultures_detail_02/Sting / CC BY-SA (http://creativecommons.org/licenses/by-sa/3.0/)/wikimedia commons; 6c1/Ram_in_the_thicket_(2)/Torquatus / CC BY-SA (https://creativecommons.org/licenses/by-sa/4.0)/wikimedia commons; 6cr/The_thrones_and_palaces_of_Babylon_and_Nineveh_from_sea_to_sea__a_thousand_miles_on_horseback_(1876)_(14591496557)/Internet Archive Book Images / No restrictions/wikimedia commons; 6bl/Gudea_of_Lagash_Girsu/Louvre Museum / Public domain/wikimedia commons; 6br/Ur_mosaic/Alma E. Guinness / CC0/wikimedia commons; 7tr/Marduk-apla-iddina_II//wikimedia commons; 7cr1/Nimrud_Ivory_lion_eating_a_man/Prioryman / CC BY-SA (https://creativecommons.org/licenses/by-sa/3.0)/wikimedia commons; 7cr/A_glazed_terracotta_tile_from Nimrud,_/Osama Shukir Muhammed Amin FRCP(Glasg) / CC BY-SA (https://creativecommons.org/licenses/by-sa/4.0)/wikimedia commons; 8tl/CairoEgMuseumTaaMaskMostlyPhotographed/Roland Unger / CC BY-SA (https://creativecommons.org/licenses/by-sa/3.0)/wikimedia commons; 8tc/File:SFEC-L-ABYDOS11.JPG/Steve F-E-Cameron / CC BY-SA (https://creativecommons.org/licenses/by-sa/3.0)/wikimedia commons; 8tr/Menkaura/King_Menkaura_(Mycerinus)_and_queen.jpg: Unknown carver. Photo by Jenderivative work: Gospodar svemira / CC BY-SA (https://creativecommons.org/licenses/by-sa/3.0)/wikimedia commons; 8c/Gaming Board Inscribed for Amenhotep_III_with_Separate_Sliding_Drawer,_ca._1390-1353_B.C.E.,49.56a-b/Charles Edwin Wilbour Fund / No restrictions/wikimedia commons; 8br1/Tutankhamun_scarab1/https://www.flickr.com/photos/dalbera/ / CC BY (https://creativecommons.org/licenses/by/2.0)/wikimedia commons; 8br2/Keramik-Neues-Museum-02/Didia / CC BY-SA (https://creativecommons.org/licenses/by-sa/3.0)/wikimedia commons; 9tr/File:Weighing of the heart3.jpg/Hunefer / Public domain/wikimedia commons; 9cl/Medio_regno,_XII-XVII_dinastia,_ippopotamo_in_faience,_1938-1539_ac_ca._01/Sailko / CC BY (https://creativecommons.org/licenses/by/3.0)/wikimedia commons; 9c/Louvre_calice_forme_nenuphar/Louvre Museum / CC BY-SA (http://creativecommons.org/licenses/by-sa/3.0/)/wikimedia commons; 9cr/Applique_in_faience_per_tempietti_in_legno,_periodo_tolemaico,_falco 05/Sailko / CC BY (https://creativecommons.org/licenses/by/3.0)/wikimedia commons, 9bl/The_Judgement_of_the_dead_in_the_presence_of_Osiris/Hunefer / Public domain/wikimedia commons; 10tr/Sialk_pot_(cropped)/Original uploader and creator was Zereshk at en.wikipedia / CC BY-SA (http://creativecommons.org/licenses/by-sa/3.0/)/wikimedia commons; 10tl1/Elam_cool//wikimedia commons; 10tl2/Plaque,_probably_a_clothing_attachment,_Northern_Iran,_possibly_/Daderot / CC0/wikimedia commons; 10c/Standard_Finial_LACMA_M.76.97.90/Los Angeles County Museum of Art / Public domain/wikimedia commons; 10cr1/Forehead_ornament_for_/Daderot / CC0/wikimedia commons; 10cl/Gold_Rhyton_in_the_form_of_a_Ram_s Head - Reza Abbasi_Museum_-_Tehran,_Iran/A Davey from Portland, Oregon, EE UU / CC BY (https://creativecommons.org/licenses/by/2.0)/wikimedia commons; 10cr1/Zwei_Protome,_Armreif_und_Silberschale_mit Goldauflagen_aus_Ziwiye_in_Iran,_c.a._8._Jh._v.C//wikimedia commons; 10br/Achaemenid_gold_ornaments,70.142.6-.11/Unknown artists / No restrictions/wikimedia commons; 10br1/Nowruz_Zoroastrian/Ipaat at English Wikipedia / CC BY-SA (https://creativecommons.org/licenses/by-sa/3.0)/wikimedia commons; 11tl/Sphinx_Darius_Louvre/Louvre Museum / Public domain/wikimedia commons; 11tc1/Armlet_from_the_Oxus_Treasure_BM_1897.12-31.116/© Marie-Lan Nguyen / Wikimedia Commons/wikimedia commons; 11tc1/Gold_fish_shaped_vessel_from_the_Oxus_Treasure_by_Nickmard_Khoey/British Museum / CC BY-SA (https://creativecommons.org/licenses/by-sa/2.0)/wikimedia commons; 11tr/File:Scythiancarpet.jpg/See page for author / Public domain/wikimedia commons; 11cr/Persepolis carvings/By Matt Amery/wikimedia commons; 11bl/Coupole,Kakrak._Bamiyan.Mus/Ismoon (talk) 17:54, 27 December 2012 (UTC) / CC0/wikimedia commons; 11bc/Anahita Vessel, 300-500 AD, Sasanian, Iran, silver and gilt - Cleveland Museum of Art - DSC08129.JPG/Daderot / CC0/wikimedia commons; 11br1/MIK_-_Sassaniden_Eber/Wolfgang Sauber / CC BY-SA (https://creativecommons.org/licenses/by-sa/3.0)/wikimedia commons; 11br2/Iran_sasanide,_coppa_ovale_in_argento_con_sogg._vegetali_e_geometrici,_VII_sec (1)/I, Sailko / CC BY-SA (https://creativecommons.org/licenses/by-sa/3.0)/wikimedia commons; 12tl/Akrotiri_minoan_town/unknown minoan artist / Public domain/wikimedia commons; 12tr/Reconstructed_Minoan_Fresco_Avaris/Martin Dürrschnabel / CC BY-SA (https://creativecommons.org/licenses/by-sa/2.5)/wikimedia commons; 12cl/File:Minoan snake goddess.JPG/Soverylittlehoneybee / CC BY-SA (https://creativecommons.org/licenses/by-sa/4.0)/wikimedia commons; 12cl1/Minoan_craft_-_golden_bee/Andree Stephan / CC BY (https://creativecommons.org/licenses/by/3.0)/wikimedia commons; 12cr1/Marching_soldiers_observed_by_a_female_figure,_In_a_krater_of_c._1200_BC_in_Mycenae/Self picture / CC BY (https://creativecommons.org/licenses/by/3.0)/wikimedia commons; 12cr2/Vafeio_Mycenaen_laconian/Putinovac / Public domain/wikimedia commons; 12c/Minoan_Plate/O.Mustafin / CC0/wikimedia commons; 12bl/AMI_-_Stierrhyton/Wolfgang Sauber / CC BY-SA (https://creativecommons.org/licenses/by-sa/3.0)/wikimedia commons; 12bc/Minoan_bull_leaper/British Museum / CC BY-SA (https://creativecommons.org/licenses/by-sa/3.0)/wikimedia commons; 12br/Fresco on a wall of Throne Room a at Knossos Archeological Site in Crete, Greece/By cybervelvet/wikimedia commons; 13tr/Knossos_fresco_women/cavorite / CC BY-SA (https://creativecommons.org/licenses/by-sa/2.0)/wikimedia commons; 13c/Minoan_Master_of_Animals_jewellery/British Museum / CC BY-SA (https://creativecommons.org/licenses/by-sa/4.0)/wikimedia commons; 13cr1/Rock_crystal_rhyton_archmus_Heraklion/Heraklion Archaeological Museum / Public domain/wikimedia commons; 13cr2/Small_golden_double_head_minoan_axe_archmus_Heraklion/Heraklion Archaeological Museum / CC0/wikimedia commons; 13bl/Tonkrug_Phaistos_01/Olaf Tausch / CC BY (https://creativecommons.org/licenses/by/3.0)/wikimedia commons; 13bc/Kamares_ware,_AMH,_144912/Zde / CC BY-SA (https://creativecommons.org/licenses/by-sa/4.0)/wikimedia commons; 13br/Minoan_larnax,_cattle,_Crete,_AMH,_145321/Zde / CC BY-SA (https://creativecommons.org/licenses/by-sa/4.0)/wikimedia commons; 14cl/Stag_hunt_mosaic,_Pella/Unknown author / Public domain/wikimedia commons; 14c/Ancient greek vase isolated on white with clipping path/By Kamira/wikimedia commons; 14cr/Exekias_Dionysos_Staatliche_Antikensammlungen_2044/Exekias / CC BY-SA (http://creativecommons.org/licenses/by-sa/3.0/)/wikimedia commons; 14bl/Ancient greek vase depicting a chariot isolated on white with clipping path/By Kamira/wikimedia commons; 15tl/0_Monument_funeÝ□raire_-_Adonis_mourant_-_Museu_Gregoriano_Etrusco/Vatican Museums / CC BY-SA (https://creativecommons.org/licenses/by-sa/3.0)/wikimedia commons; 15tc/Marble statue of Kroisos Kouros (530 B.C.), found at Anavyssos, Attica./By Lefteris Papaulakis/wikimedia commons; 15tr/Medea_-_Casa_dei_Dioscuri/Naples National Archaeological Museum / Public domain/wikimedia commons; 15b/The_Blinding_of_Polyphemus,_cast_reconstruction_of_the_group,_Sperlonga_(14969535228)/Carole Raddato from FRANKFURT, Germany / CC BY-SA (https://creativecommons.org/licenses/by-sa/2.0)/wikimedia commons; 16tl/Ludovisi_Gaul_Altemps_Inv8608_n3/Museo nazionale romano di palazzo Altemps / Public domain/wikimedia commons; 16tc/Affresco_romano_-_eracle_ed_onfale_-_area_vesuviana/Stefano Bolognini / Attribution/wikimedia commons; 16tr2/VerlovingAureliusFaustina/CharlesS at Dutch Wikipedia / CC BY-SA (http://creativecommons.org/licenses/by-sa/3.0/)/wikimedia commons; 16cr/Great_Cameo_of_France_CdM_Paris_Bab264_white_background/ Cabinet des Médailles / CC BY-SA (http://creativecommons.org/licenses/by-sa/3.0/)/wikimedia commons; 16br/Pompeii_-_Casa_dei_Vettii_-_Ixion/WolfgangRieger / Public domain/wikimedia commons; 17bl/Old_man_vatican_pushkin01/shakko / CC BY-SA (https://creativecommons.org/licenses/by-sa/3.0)/wikimedia commons; 17tl/Battle of Issus mosaic - Museo Archeologico Nazionale - Naples 2013-05-16 16-25-06 BW.jpg/Berthold Werner / Public domain/wikimedia commons; 17tr/05-Mosaico_del_Oecus._Aquiles_en_Skyros_alta/Anonymous mosaic artist from late Roman Spain, active during the late 4th-5th centuries AD / Public domain/wikimedia commons; 17cr/File:-0030 Grabrelief Publius Aiedius Amphio und Frau Aiedia Altes Museum anagoria.JPG/Altes Museum / CC BY (https://creativecommons.org/licenses/by/3.0)/wikimedia commons; 17bl/File:Old man vatican pushkin01.jpg/shakko / CC BY-SA (https://creativecommons.org/licenses/by-sa/3.0)/wikimedia commons; 18tl/Alhambra de Granada. Moorish arches in the Court of the Lions/By Jose Ignacio Soto/wikimedia commons; 18tr/IlkhanateSilkCircular/unknown / (of the reproduction) Davids Samling, Copenhagen / Public domain/wikimedia commons; 18c/Samarkand_Shah-i_Zinda_Tuman_Aqa_complex_cropped2/User:Patrickringgenberg / CC BY (https://creativecommons.org/licenses/by/3.0)/wikimedia commons; 18cr/WLA_vanda_Ottoman_marquetry_and_tile-top_table_2/Wikipedia Loves Art participant "VeronikaB" / CC BY (https://creativecommons.org/licenses/by/2.5)/wikimedia commons; 18br1/Mantes_carpet_Louvre_OA6610_detail1/Louvre Museum / Public domain/wikimedia commons; 18br/Pyxid_Al_Mughira_OA_4068/Louvre Museum / Public domain/wikimedia commons; 19tl/:Фаррух Бек Бабур принимает придворных. Бабурнаме. 1589. Гал. Саклера,

Modern Architecture

Inside

Modern Art

Inside

Renaissance Architecture

Inside

Renaissance Art

Inside